Praise for

THE FAMILY BANKING BLUEPRINT

Christin is a *genius* in wealth building through real estate, with an incredible ability to simplify complex concepts and make them actionable for anyone. Her authenticity and genuine heart for helping others build wealth set her apart as more than just an expert—she's a true advocate for your success. Her synergy with her grandmother's wisdom adds a powerful, multigenerational depth to her proven approach. Relatable and impactful, Christin is the best friend you need to build lasting wealth and legacy. Plus, the rich resources embedded in this book will not just serve as critical knowledge but as actionable steps to start today!

Tamra Andress,
Business Coach & Movement Maker,Podcaster, Author & Speaker

Christin is a true beacon of faith and light, living out her commitment to God in every aspect of her life. Her inspiring book is a testament to her ability to uplift and guide others, offering profound wisdom and practical insights. Each chapter builds upon timeless truths, weaving together the beauty of God's design with actionable steps to live a purposeful life.

Christin's writing is both empowering and deeply relatable. Her emphasis on Balance, Passion, and even practical topics, like Real Estate Investing and Family Banking, speaks to her holistic approach to life and finances.

Christin doesn't just inspire; she equips others to live with intention, make an impact, and align their lives with God's greater plan. Her work is a must-read for anyone seeking to grow spiritually, personally, and professionally.

Kyle Fuller,

Christin Kingsbury delivers a powerful roadmap for building wealth and living life with intention. Her focus on designing a life around your talents, priorities, and relationships makes this book relatable and inspiring. If you're ready to embrace financial freedom while creating a meaningful legacy, this is the guide you need!

Kristen Cantrell,
Wife, Mother, Community Builder, Realtor, Podcaster, Airbnb Super Host

The Family Banking Blueprint is more than just a financial guide—it's a roadmap for designing a life of intention, financial freedom, and generational wealth. Through her powerful insights on mindset, talent, and purpose, Christin masterfully blends practical strategies with wisdom, empowering readers to build businesses, lead boldly, and live abundantly. This book isn't just about finances; it's about creating a legacy and embracing life's greatest adventures with purpose and clarity.

Kevin Kauffman,
Co-Founder of Group 4610 & Next Level Agents Podcast/Network

The Family Banking Blueprint is a transformational guide for those ready to break free from limiting beliefs about money and embrace a life of purpose, passion, and generational impact. Christin Kingsbury brilliantly combines actionable financial strategies with heart-centered wisdom, inspiring us to use our God-given talents to build true freedom—not just for ourselves but for those we love and serve. This is more than a book; it's a roadmap to creating a life by design, where abundance flows and legacies are born.

Glenn Lundy,
Husband, Father of Eight, Motivational Speaker,
and Founder of 800% Elite Automotive Club

Christin's book is incredibly insightful for anyone looking to build the life they want! She gives incredible practical insight into how to grow wealth, create a life of freedom, live generously, and open your eyes to what's possible when you take the steps to make it happen! This is not just a book but a blueprint for anyone who wants to live life by design! I cannot recommend it enough!

Melissa Lea Hughes,
Speaker, Podcaster, Social Media Influencer,
and CEO of Rise Social Media Agency

This book is an inspiring and practical guide for entrepreneurs—especially moms—who want to break free from the rat race and build a life of financial freedom and purpose. With insightful worksheets, real-world tools, and a mindset shift toward abundance, it equips readers to use their talents wisely, create passive income, and build a legacy that blesses their families and others. A must-read for anyone ready to rethink money, embrace adventure, and step boldly into their God-given potential!

Krystal J. Parker,
President of the U.S. Christian Chamber of Commerce,
Business Strategist, Best-Selling Author, and Host of *The Shepherd at Work*

It is my honor to recommend Christin Kingsbury's book on family, banking, real estate, and generational wealth-building principles. This book beautifully intertwines the author's values and her commitment to teaching others the rules around building wealth that she learned through family banking, real estate, and long-term family wealth strategies in order to not just merely succeed but to become a transformational leader who leaves a powerful legacy.

Kristan Cole,
Owner of Kristan Cole Network,
Keller Williams Operating Partner, Speaker, and Teacher

Christin Kingsbury absolutely nails it in *The Family Banking Blueprint*! This book is like a blueprint for turning your God-given talents into a life of financial freedom, joy, and purpose. Her down-to-earth wisdom and step-by-step guidance make building generational wealth feel not only possible but exciting and deeply meaningful. If you're ready to design a life of impact, profitability, and adventure, this is your roadmap!

Mindy Backsen,
Top Social Selling Leader, Mentor, and Coach

Money can feel like a big, scary monster, but Christin Kingsbury breaks it down in a way that makes building wealth simple, doable, and even exciting. *The Family Banking Blueprint* is the roadmap you didn't know you needed to take control of your finances, leverage your talents, and create a life of true abundance. If you're ready to stop letting money control you and start mastering it, this book is your game-changer!

Brindley Tucker,
CEO of Your Realty Leverage, Inc.

If you've ever felt like financial freedom was out of reach, and you're working hard but never quite getting ahead, then this book is your roadmap to changing that forever. Christin has taken what so many overcomplicate and made it simple, clear, and actionable. This isn't just theory. It is a proven, step-by-step guide to building lasting wealth through real estate and, more importantly, securing your family's financial future for generations to come. Read it, apply it, and watch your life change.

Carin Nguyen,
Best-Selling Author, Entrepreneur & Wealth Builder

Simplifying
Real Estate Investing
To Build Generational
Wealth!

THE
FAMILY
BANKING
BLUEPRINT

Christin Kingsbury

The Family Banking Blueprint:
Simplifying Real Estate Investing To Build Generational Wealth
Copyright 2025 Christin Kingsbury
ISBN (paperback) 978-1-7379022-8-7
ISBN (hardcover) 979-8-9928101-3-4
ISBN (e-book) 979-8-9928101-2-7

Published by F.I.T. in Faith Press

F. I.T.

PRESS

THIS BOOK IS DEDICATED TO...

my Grandma Clare, whose experiences and stories you'll find handwritten throughout this book. She is the backbone and matriarch of our family and a light in the lives of so many others she has inspired and helped through the storms of life. She has taught me that I am capable of absolutely anything I put my mind to and that one person's life can make a massive impact on the lives of others. She has encouraged me to never fear what lies ahead but to believe in myself and walk through it. She has shown me that building massive wealth with just my brains and relationships is possible if I believe it's possible.

What a woman! She is still blessing my life and the lives of so many others as she approaches one hundred years old. Together, we have gone on once-in-a-lifetime adventures few people will ever experience, and the wealth she built is still funding her travels and adventures today. As I write this, she finished a lunch date with my cousin in a driverless car and is off on a six-week adventure to India! She is still investing, creating passive income, blessing others, traveling, and learning. She believes in **living** until she dies (her words) and has taught me to do the same.

TABLE OF CONTENTS

ACKNOWLEDGMENTS

I AM GRATEFUL FOR MY FAMILY, WHO listened to me and gave me quiet time to put these thoughts on paper; for the beautiful kiddos and husband, who walked this journey out and held the paint brushes as we ate pizza on the floor and made flipping houses a family affair, one-year-old included; and for my loving mother and grandmother, who showed me vastly different perspectives of what was possible and who loses if I don't win.

Thank you to my close friends and mentors, Steve Chader and Ben Kinney, who have gone before me, loved me through life's crazy moments, pushed me to keep going, and taught me the importance of wealth building. To Don and Carol, who showed me that you don't need to know someone to bless them in ways that will forever change their life and the lives of their kids. To Glenn, for introducing me to exceptional people, like Tamra Andress, who inspired me and made me believe this is a message that will bless many—a message that needed to be in a book.

And to God, the one who knows the challenge and the lesson before I see it, the one who provides every time and allows me to be a steward of the financial blessings within my reach, the one who gifted me with a message that will help others on their mission.

Never did I think I'd write a book, but thank you all for contributing to the life, character, and impact I am living out.

FOREWORD

Money isn't complicated.

SMALL STEPS. Big results over time. The tough part for most of us is that we have trouble taking those small steps—saving up for a down payment on a home, getting rid of debt, controlling our expenses, opening a retirement account, or simply figuring out where to invest the money we've saved or how to earn a better return. The changes seem complicated, and the options seem limitless. The information coming at us is overwhelming. We think most options are too complex or too risky. A friend of a friend once said, "I'd choose to do almost anything rather than spend time figuring out a financial plan. I just have no idea where to start."

I've been there.

I spent years of my life feeling confused, overwhelmed, and a little ashamed of some of my financial choices, always afraid that I might screw up or make a bad decision. No matter how bad things got, the scariest thing I could imagine was not my current situation but the idea of waking up in five years to find that nothing had changed. The thought of continuing to work so hard, only to see no progress, was just too painful for me to fathom.

Honestly, I just got tired of worrying. This was especially true after one particularly rough year. So I started reading books. I took classes and went to seminars. I talked to accountants and financial advisors, hired experts, and found wealthy mentors. Year by year, I felt a little less confused, a little less lost. I began to see a path through the fog, but I was surprised by how long it took.

I also realized that most of the financial models I was taught were either too complicated or exclusive (meaning I didn't personally qualify for some

I attended often made me feel a little uneasy—as if I were about to be sold something or those involved were working on commission.

I've read hundreds of books about money and investing, the stock market, business success stories, real estate investing, taxes, trusts, life insurance, and retirement accounts. As I read, I began to realize that the retirement books were written by stock brokers or people who owned financial companies, and the life insurance books were written by life insurance salespeople. Similarly, the business and leadership books were written by people who had amazing success in their specific businesses. This observation wasn't necessarily a bad thing; in fact, it led me to write this foreword. I found that Christin's book offers the simplest solution to becoming wealthy—FREEDOM. Having this book earlier in my journey would have saved me thousands of hours of research, pain, and worry.

At the end of the day, we all want a plan that can withstand the toughest of times and grow into something that sets us free financially. This book is that plan. It's not a hypothetical read or a feel-good book; instead, it lays out a simple plan for steadily and consistently growing your wealth, year after year.

If you're always worried about money and unsure of what next year will look like, this book can help. If you feel financially stable but you're not really getting ahead, this book can help. If you're doing pretty well but aren't confident you're making the best financial decisions to reach your goals, this book can help. It's like a recipe, and like all good recipes, it's based on extensive research, decades of trial and error, and simplifying, simplifying, simplifying. In addition, you can customize it based on what works for you. (Some people like nuts in their cookies, and some don't.) By the end of this book, you will have learned some simple models that you can use to develop your recipe—your own simple plan—for becoming wealthier in the coming year and beyond.

Christin is not offering a magic pill, a get-rich-quick scheme, or a secret for picking stocks. She isn't planning to shame you, scare you, or demand that you do exactly what she did. Instead, she will tell you about the financial essentials, the habits, the leadership lessons, and the simple models that will eventually become your own financial recipe. They are based on what she has personally implemented and what she has learned by studying others who are not only wealthy but amazing humans.

The first step is to believe that small changes and a simple plan can create massive results over time. As one of my mentors said, "People often overestimate what they can accomplish in the short term and underestimate what they can do over time." In other words, your wealth is within reach—if you have a plan and follow it.

Learning to get right with money has greatly affected me and the people in my world. Over a handful of years, I've had the honor of building a company that produces over 400 million dollars in revenue annually and employs 1,100 employees and over 5,000 independent contractors. The shift in my knowledge of money has taken me from a negative net worth to one that has allowed me to give to causes, invest in people, and create many millionaires who pay it forward and have a compounding ripple effect on families and the world.

I have known Christin as a close friend and business partner for many years and can vouch for her as a teacher and as an amazing human being. So do me a favor: Read this book cover to cover, do the homework, use the worksheets, and trust the process. I have 100 percent confidence that Christin will change your life—if you let her.

Ben Kinney
Founder of PLACE

PREFACE

I'VE ALWAYS BEEN VERY MINDFUL THAT I only get to do this thing called life once, and what I do with it impacts the generations that follow me more than I could ever imagine. I believed and created a life that allows me to pick up the kids from school, eat dinner each night with my family, take three-day weekends to travel and adventure with loved ones, and enjoy a life that is debt and mortgage-free—all with what others call "mailbox money." I was told it was impossible, but I just didn't believe I was confined by the limiting beliefs of others. Instead, I went on a mission to build and have what they said I couldn't.

I'm a woman of great faith, and it's gotten me through some incredibly hard times. My children and my husband mean the world to me. When I found Mike, I didn't have much experience with functional relationships or with husbands who could truly be the rock and support their wives needed as they journeyed through life's challenges. Instead, I had witnessed the chaos of what dysfunctional relationships could do to families and the danger and fear that could be experienced as a kid when dysfunctional relationships and low income crossed paths.

As Mike and I started our life together, I vowed to be an awesome partner, a present mother, a faithful follower, and living proof of a loving God. All I ever wanted was a boy and a girl, and we went through losing many to gain the beautiful babies we got to keep. It was hard, and it took faith, grit, and belief that God had promised us more, and we were going to claim it!

In less time than I had ever imagined, I built a small million-dollar real estate team and partnered with some of the most brilliant minds in the industry, even when others told me it was literally impossible. Through relationships, creative financing, and sweat equity (not some pot of money we had lying around), we acquired brokerages and title companies, short-

and held multifamily properties, flipped single-family homes, developed land, and built spec homes. Currently, I'm building out a destination campground and retreat center. With more than twenty-one rentals, the cash flow from our investment properties is over six figures annually, giving us peace of mind and the freedom to experience life and bless others the way we always imagined and we're only getting started.

I'm insanely passionate about the security and opportunity passive income brings to families. During good times and bad, it offers peace to whether the storm and leverage to multiply abundance. We have built a multimillion-dollar net worth, carry zero consumer debt, hold only assets that pay for themselves (all generating income twice the cost of owning them), and coauthored a best seller on integrating faith, family, and passive income. I teach others to get out of debt, create multiple streams of income, and use their finances to be a blessing to others. I believe that educating people to make new choices around money can break old poverty mindsets and build generational wealth.

Today, my companies work to fund financial and business education for at-risk kids and provide education to moms around the world who want to change the trajectory of their family bloodline, live intentionally present, and enjoy an abundant life.

INTRODUCTION

AS YOU JOURNEY THROUGH THIS BOOK, MY goal is to get you thinking outside the box about ways to live out your dreams and be intentional about being, doing, and becoming all you have imagined in this one life you are blessed with. You will read words of wisdom and stories written by my grandmother, telling of her more than ninety-eight years of building an abundant life on this earth, as well as more current stories and lessons of my own about obstacles I have faced and opportunities I have taken. My hope is that you will see that you don't have to be the smartest, richest, or luckiest to create the life you've dreamed of and find the happiness and fulfillment you desire. You just have to have clarity on what you want, a tiny belief that it could be you, and the motivation to consistently do the next best step.

> You just have to have clarity on what you want, a tiny belief that it could be you, and the motivation to consistently do the next best step.

As you read, you'll find stories of joy and pain, excitement and disappointment, blessings and challenges, and actionable activities to move your life in the right direction using simple tools and hacks I have employed along the way. This book is a reminder that life is a journey, not a destination, and you can truly be grateful and blessed as you climb the highest mountains or walk through the darkest valleys. It's a reminder that every day is a challenge meant to grow you or break you. It's a lesson that anything is possible, and wealth can be acquired regardless of whether you were born with it or had to work for it. It's a reflection on the truths that money is not the root of all evil and that relationships and integrity generate wealth, contrary to the things you may have been taught. It consists of lessons that span almost one hundred years and three generations, written mother and myself. I hope you find it inspiring, funny, educational, and impactful, and my sincere hope is that it crushes the limiting belief that is holding you back—the belief that it can't be you. If it can be me, it *can* be you. God intended you to live an abundant life and bless those around you. Go be a blessing!

Chapter 1

BY DESIGN

Create a life by *design*, not by default.

YOU CAN LITERALLY HAVE ANYTHING YOU WANT in life if you believe it and are willing to do the work. The beauty of life is it can be anything you want it to be. You can create it anywhere in the world. You can surround yourself with amazing people. You can have the career you love with a schedule that supports your goals. Yet, these truths are not something people recognize as fact, so they become reactive to life and tend to choose the path of least resistance. But the path of least resistance still requires work. It demands your time, includes challenges, and requires effort. So, if you're guaranteed the struggle, why not fight to build the life you love? Push through; those battle scars are proof that you won and fought hard for the amazing life you created.

Creating life on your terms requires clarity of "what" your terms are. Is it a life where you can afford what you want when you want? Does it allow you adventures and experiences for yourself and your family? Will it afford you the opportunity to be the light financially and bless others with as little or as much as you have to give? Life by design requires a proactive approach, not a reactive approach. It requires you to ask yourself the hard questions. It requires you to build a plan and gain clarity, identifying the next challenge that will grow you. It will require you to become the person your dreams require. The steps will become clear, but the path must be intentional.

> Creating life on your terms requires clarity of "what" your terms are.

Chapter 2

RELATIONSHIPS

The wealth is in the *relationships*.

FIND MENTORS IN THE AREAS WHERE YOU WANT TO GROW, AND DON'T BE AFRAID TO BE NEW AT SOMETHING.

"Although I had a master's degree, I knew next to nothing about financing houses, qualifying clients for bank loans, selling land, finding legal corners of a property, or writing legal descriptions accurately. It was a new learning challenge. I particularly remember an older ranch [specialist] who was appalled at my ignorance regarding writing legal descriptions. He took the time to teach me. I also took classes and read. As time passed and all three kids were in school all day, I enrolled in certified commercial investment courses taught by the National Association of Realtors. The courses were rigorous. They were taught in different cities in the U.S., and to qualify for their designation, it was required to have sold commercial real estate and to write a thesis showing the implementation of CCIM [Certified Commercial Investment Member] techniques. It took me several years, and it gave me the self-confidence to trust myself. I became the first female CCIM in Arizona. That was fun; I loved breaking into the "good old boys' club!"

—Grandma Clare

THE SECRET TO THE JOURNEY OF BUILDING an abundant life is relationships. You don't have time for everyone. Some people bring more joy and energy than others. Audit the relationships around you. Whose names would come to mind if you had to identify your most valued relationships? Who would they be if that were only a small group of people? Who will get the most of you on this journey? Who would you choose to spend most of your time impacting, loving, and experiencing life with?

> Who will get the most of you on this journey?

Consider the relationships that make you a better person. They say you are the average of the five people you spend the most time with—the average of their character, their knowledge, their values, and even the average of their bank accounts. Read that again; that may be your first problem! If the average of your mentors and friends is lower than that of someone living the life, you desire, you need to raise your standards and upgrade your relationships. Be intentional and make time for your relationships. Seek out people in the world who share your values and your goals—people who have done the things you want to do. Seek to learn so much about them that you gain value through your studies and add value back to their lives. That's how great lifelong relationships are born. Don't assume you will find one person who can mentor and help you grow through all areas of your life. Some people have talents in finance, while others excel in parenting, physical health, relationships, spirituality, or even business. Expecting one person to teach you all things sets you up for disappointment and will likely ruin the relationship.

Seek relationships from people winning in the following areas: (1) faith, (2) family, (3) finance, (4) fun, (5) career/business, (6) health, (7) relationships, and (8) growth **(REFER TO THE AMAZING MENTORS RESOURCE AT THE END OF THE CHAPTER)**. Understand that a single relationship has the power to change your life forever. Remember that and be intentional about finding and nurturing your connections.

> Understand that a single relationship has the power to change your life forever.

When my husband and I were just kids and wanted to start our own business, we hadn't a clue, nor did we have the funds to get started.

ethic, trustworthiness, and good character. My husband completed a small remodel job for a man who saw those qualities in him. Don was an older gentleman who had worked hard to build wealth for his family. He appreciated a kid with work ethic. He had lost his son to an accident at my husband's age, and their relationship became one that filled a void for Don and offered mentorship to Mike.

> Have a goals for the future, but don't live in them to the point that you can't appreciate the present.

This one relationship funded our start-up construction business. I had only met Don for fifteen minutes when he deposited $300,000 in our bank account! That money funded the construction of a home, which gave our family work and profited us greatly. We put in the sweat equity, and Don put in the funds. That relationship changed our family forever. That one relationship, built by just showing up and doing a good job, has since greatly benefited our family and Don's. He passed shortly after, and we have since made it a priority to ensure that his wife is safe and cared for because he cared so deeply for us in the short time we knew him. People we hardly knew changed our financial future for generations moving forward! Over time, relationships such as this have helped us build a great net worth, allowing us to pay off houses and cars and enjoy a life with no consumer debt at an early age. These relationships have also afforded us the opportunity to pay it forward, creating opportunities for others.

Never underestimate the importance of a single relationship! Always show up as your best; people are watching, even when you are unaware. Model hard work and high integrity, and don't waste time being concerned about being judged. Instead, show up as someone you

> Show up as someone you can be proud of at the end of your life.

can be proud of at the end of your life. It may literally have the power to

Amazing MENTORS

You are the average of the people you spend the most time with. Not one person can mentor you in all areas. Who will you intentionally grow with this year? List those strongest in the following areas...

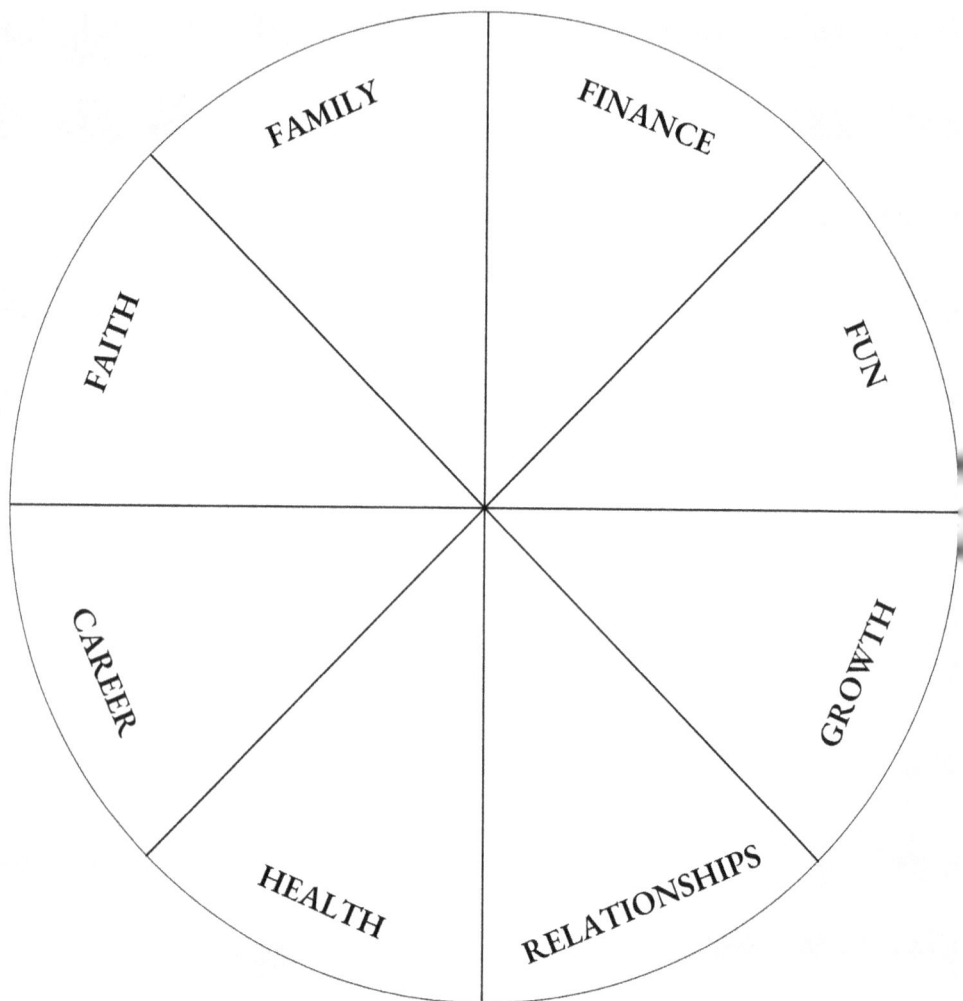

FAMILY

FINANCE

FAITH

FUN

CAREER

GROWTH

HEALTH

RELATIONSHIPS

Chapter 3

BALANCE

Shoot for counterbalance because *balance* is a unicorn.

AT ITS BEST, A LIFE BY DESIGN is well-rounded. Although it will never be balanced in all areas at the exact same moment, you will know you're winning when you have a good handle on *counterbalancing* several of the eight areas discussed in chapter two (faith, family, finance, fun, career/business, health, relationships, and growth).

Life can feel like a washing machine at times. You'll get thrown in one direction or another over the years, but remember, it's not about perfect balance. It's about recognizing when life's out of whack and then counterbalancing to the best of your ability. Use the Road of Life worksheet often to assess where you are out of balance and in need of adjustment

Remember to savor the moments. Be present and experience the pain and the joy; experience the people you're with. Truly soak in the uniqueness and the lessons of the people you're blessed to spend your moments with. Over the years, I have learned that when you focus on everything you *have* to be grateful for, you'll never *need* anything! Have goals for the future, but don't live in them to the point you can't appreciate the present. Learn from the past, but don't have your eyes focused there. Be excited for what's to come, but don't ignore the joy in the moment. Life is about being in and learning from the current moment. It's about the journey and the growth along the way, not the destination. The wealth in life is found in the relationships you build and the experiences you create.

Take time to look back at the years of your life and how far you have come as you work to design the future you love. What have been your natural talents all along, your God-given gifts? What things have given you energy? What are the things you would show up and do, even if there were no compensation offered? What have others told you you do well? What have you done well in the past? What makes you smile and adds energy to your life? Even the little things matter here. I encourage you to sit in a quiet space and take some time to make a list of all the people and things that bring you joy. List the things you love down to the tiniest detail, like the sound of birds and the warm sun on your skin. Write down the people you want to impact. What do you want them to say about you when they celebrate who you were at the end of your life? These people and things should be prioritized in your calendar moving forward.

Road of *LIFE*

Assess your level of fulfillment and the amount of attention you're devoting to each area on a scale from 1 to 10 and shade the arrows accordingly.

1	FAITH	10
1	FAMILY	10
1	FINANCE	10
1	FUN	10
1	GROWTH	10
1	RELATIONSHIPS	10
1	HEALTH	10
1	CAREER	10

Chapter 4

ENVIRONMENT

Create an *environment* of self-care.

THE IDEA OF BUILDING WEALTH AND ABUNDANCE goes hand in hand with your environment. In a busy world full of chaos, your life needs some white noise, some time to think, and some time just for you. This is especially true if you're a busy working momma or daddy.

In life, putting other people and things ahead of yourself on the priority list is easy, and "think time" is often missing altogether. Adding think time is one slight shift that will change your world and help you move the ball forward. Build a bunker; your private think space is sacred. Sometimes, that means getting up at 5:00 a.m. to process thoughts on a project, reflect on the day ahead, learn something, journal, exercise, or just be with God. It's the time when kids and dogs are still sleeping, husbands are not awake enough to say much, and you can just have "you" time. I challenge you to do something for yourself each time you say yes to doing something for someone else, even if it's just fifteen minutes of quiet "you" time to watch the sunrise. The restoration will compound, and you'll have more energy to give.

The way you start your morning determines your day. I fully believe that! I remember mornings as a kid when we were not ready. There was no space for preparation, no quiet time to get our minds in a good place for the day, just chaos and fighting as we ran out the door chasing our tails! Day after day, this will wear on you. Some mornings will just go that way, but it shouldn't be all of them!

> The way you start your morning determines your day.

I hope you will take the time to realize the power of prep time—mental prep time, meal prep time, and work prep time. It will change your world when you learn to cut distractions, shut off the noise, and just focus. Focus on your thoughts. Strategize and prioritize. Schedule regular bunker time on some days for your finances and on other days for addressing other important matters such as investment goals, continuing education, budgeting, and health. Learn to manage your time and prioritize yourself and your goals. Without a happy, healthy you, the ones you love get robbed of the best version of you.

I used to tell myself there was no way to escape the noise. I was so used to being busy I was addicted to it. But I changed my story and found a way.

> I used to tell myself there was no way to escape the noise. I was so used to being busy I was addicted to it. But I changed my story and found a way.

Some days, my bunker is simply being alone in my car at the park or in the garage while the kids and family run crazy in the house. Sometimes, I go to my office and lock the door so no one knows I'm there. White-noise time can be your most valuable asset in a world of family, clients, and business partners.

Chapter 5

ENERGY

Just like a magnet, your *energy* attracts your opportunities.

YOUR ENVIRONMENT AND HOW IT MAKES YOU feel influences your energy, which, in turn, impacts how you show up in this world and who you attract. Your physical and mental energy plays a massive role in your progress, and learning to control your energy and prioritize your physical and mental health are important keys to your success.

Learn ways to recognize the highs and lows in your energy and create hacks so you can easily add the things that add energy to your day. Practicing and mastering the art of changing your mental state is a tool you will never put down once you understand it. It plays a key role in taking your time back and having time to be productive rather than reactive. It involves recognizing that you choose your thoughts and can just as easily choose to change them instantly to increase your productivity, your progress on goals, and your happiness. So find the things that give you energy and insert them into a negative moment to change your thoughts. For example, when I add silly music from my childhood to a negative mindset, call a friend to lift my spirits, or take a walk outside to clear my thoughts, I get my energy back.

Your time in this life is finite, and too many people give others control of their emotions. No one deserves that much power over you. When your mind is full of anger, fear, or anxiety, you lose momentum and slow the progress of your mission. When someone throws a wrench in your day, and you allow it to destroy your mental state, recognize first that your reaction is a choice. Then, go reclaim your energy.

Your energy is what will get you to your goals. It gives or takes from your self-confidence. It may seem to have nothing to do with wealth or building a life by design, but I promise it's one of the key magic tricks to getting where you want to go. You must believe you're enough. You must know you're uniquely made. You owe it to those who need you to show up as the person God created you to be before the world stole your childlike faith. Your experiences are not a mistake. You are perfect for your mission, but you can't move far or fast if you have thoughts, people, or an environment that sucks the gas from your tank and tells you otherwise.

> **What you focus on you find.**

Let's talk about the limiting beliefs you have right now that take from your self-confidence and keep you from building wealth and living the life you desire. What do you subconsciously say to yourself over and over again that you're now believing? People reach out to me on a daily basis with the belief that I have some magic they don't have or that there must be more to the story because building wealth couldn't be something within their reach. I have news for you; you have to start questioning the thoughts that hold you back. What you focus on, you find. As silly as that may sound, your brain will hunt for proof of what you're believing, and you'll find it! Similarly, if you believe something is possible, you will find evidence to support that, too! It all starts with your thoughts.

A few years ago, I intentionally placed myself in a group of people that completely intimidated me. These were people I admired who had built bigger businesses and made more money than I ever dreamed of making. When I signed up for this class, I fully intended to be a fly on the wall. I planned to simply soak up the knowledge and not speak. After all, what could I possibly contribute? I wasn't as smart, as talented, or as hardworking as they were. I just wasn't enough, or so I had told myself. I'm not sure where those beliefs came from or why they were still following me around as I neared the age of forty. I had no clue how much they were *not* serving me!

As I sat in the class day after day, I listened and didn't contribute nearly as much as I would have in an ordinary class. I was literally in awe of those who had built seven-, eight--, and nine-figure empires and just wanted to learn enough to become a better me. I also believed that if I worked that hard, I'd lose time with my family and kiddos. If I wanted to build the wealth they had built, it would take a major sacrifice that I was unwilling or unable to make—until one conversation changed my life.

You see, a great mentor is always listening and observing. My mentor, who was leading the class, asked me to stand in front of those amazing people and share what I had done over the years with investing. Feeling vulnerable and completely embarrassed, I agreed. As I stood there talking about all the small investments I made to build passive income over the years, I figured they would see them as insignificant. After all, I didn't have much to invest with, and I never purchased anything that would impress them. Many of the properties I purchased over the years were ones they would never have stepped foot in. I started investing at age twenty-one with just $10,000 and bought some properties with as little as $3,000 and others with only $5,000. Nothing I had done was extraordinary. All the money I invested was minimal and something anyone could have duplicated. I had simply built our family's small investment portfolio with the resources and relationships available to me at the time.

I didn't realize then that I had spoken about these investments to my mentor over the years, and he had received them differently. I didn't know that because of my passion, action, and discipline in real estate and investing, I had actually built a net worth that exceeded many of the others in the class. It was likely the *only* thing I had been disciplined about in my lifetime. Discipline was a negative word in my book and not something I bothered to see the value of at the time.

After that conversation, many people in that class called me for help with investing, and many still call to this day. They were in that class to learn from my mentor (who had done *extremely* well for himself), but they called me because I hadn't done anything they couldn't do themselves. They called me because they could relate to me and duplicate what I had done. While he was so far ahead that he was an inspiration, I was a real example they could relate to.

I realized that day my beliefs about myself were untrue. They were holding me back from blessing others and, in turn, holding them back from progressing in their abundant life. That hurt! In some ways, the value I had to offer was a perfect compliment to the lessons from our mentor that day.

While he could inspire them with the levels he had reached, I could offer them the self-belief that would allow them to take real action. I was just far enough ahead that they thought they might catch me and close enough for it to seem possible. But I knew I wouldn't be able to bless others and move forward in my purpose until I kicked those limiting beliefs forever. I would never be able to share the talents and gifts God had blessed me with if I continually believed I was unworthy and less than others.

> I would never be able to share the talents and gifts God had blessed me with if I continually believed I was unworthy and less than others.

I allowed myself to receive that lesson and cried when I reflected on it. How much progress and time had been lost? How many people had I failed to bless because I didn't see myself in the right light or had false beliefs about the sacrifice it would take? How many opportunities had they lost to build wealth, secure their retirement, and create a life by design because they believed it took more money? What actions had never been taken because *we* believed it wasn't something *we* could do?

What limiting beliefs do you have that are stealing your energy and keeping you from moving forward in your purpose? Why haven't you focused on building your financial future? What would living a life of true fulfillment, one you had the financial ability to create, do for you? I challenge you to examine those beliefs and kill the ones that don't serve you. You are a child of the Most High God, uniquely made, and I promise He loves you and knows that none of your self-sabotaging beliefs are true! As a matter of fact, He can't wait for you to see your worth and step into your purpose! He can't wait for you to share the gifts He's given you because He knows the impact they will have on others. Step up and step into your talent!

When your goals are big and bless many, they require more commitment, money, *and* energy. So, in addition to examining your limiting beliefs, take some time to audit your world, including who or what depletes your energy and your time. Sometimes, it's a person, maybe even one you love. Save time for them toward the end of your day when you have completed what you need to accomplish.

Keep in mind that you teach people how to treat you. Years ago, I found that my extended family would call me with all their problems because I was the problem solver with a flexible work schedule. I quickly realized this was not serving my mission. It took up a lot of my time and stole my positive energy, making the rest of my day a drag and nonproductive. I have had to retrain my family and friends to call me after business hours and after my priorities are complete. Oddly enough, they no longer waste my time on minutiae. They call during the day only when it's important. This has done wonders for my energy and my production.

So, if you're not enjoying interactions with people, set boundaries, retrain them, or eliminate them from your day. That doesn't mean you don't love them or need to remove them from your life. In business, that may simply mean they need to report to someone other than you. In your personal life, that may mean you need to schedule calls with them at the end of the day and premeditate a planned, positive conversation before you connect.

There is nothing wrong with wanting to surround yourself with people who add energy to your life. People can be huge energy "sucks," but so can your habits. How much TV are you watching? *What* are you watching? Garbage in, garbage out—just sayin'. Are you spending hours in other people's business on social media? It's easy to do. Cut back on the time you spend on things that just steal your time and don't add value. Replace that time with learning, relationships, or something productive. Start training those around you to do the same and lead by example. Let your spouse, coworkers, and kiddos know your goals and why you're changing your habits. My husband can be my biggest saboteur if he doesn't understand my why. After all, ice cream or a cold beer at the end of a long day should never be off-limits, right? So let them know what support you need from them to move the ball forward. Often, this means just making them aware of your scheduled think time.

Stop feeling guilty about taking time for yourself! By doing so, you're modeling great habits. When those close to you understand that they get a better version of you when they allow you space to be your best, they will be on board. Create and speak about family goals and the rewards for results. When you create family goals, and they see that the results are moving

> "Think Time" is essential to progress. Nothing kills productivity and financial gain more than being caught in the noise of the rat race.

everyone forward, they will begin to realize the power of your white-noise time and allow you to have it.

Think time is essential to progress. Nothing kills productivity and financial gain more than being caught in the noise of the rat race. Even if it's in small increments, you must have it. Create rewards for yourself and others that are based on your progress. There is no better accountability partner than a kid who wants to go to Disneyland after Mom and Dad reach their big financial goal. Let them in on the vision, encourage them to participate, and help you win! Regulating mental and emotional energy throughout the day is a game-changer for making good habits stick. By scheduling breaks, sleeping well, inviting positive people in, and eliminating negativity, you will be empowered to show up strong.

When you start going down this rabbit hole, you'll realize that you will have to start saying no to things and people in order to say yes to yourself and what fills your cup. What are you willing to say no to? Who and what will you *need* to start saying no to? What will be your non-negotiables? Focus on what you *can* control!

As women, we tend to want to take care of anyone and everyone. This may make us feel valued, but it costs us time, energy, and finances. An even greater expense is the lost opportunities that result from our inability to focus on the mission. Many of those around us have even learned that we will just do it for them if they play the helpless card. When we do this, we fail to teach them to be independent. We want to solve their problems, but instead, we rob them of the opportunity to learn to problem solve and the confidence that comes from being independent. The greatest thing we can teach those we love is to think for themselves. It's a dying skill in our world but a highly valuable one. We can't afford to deprive ourselves of valuable time that could be spent building a life that will benefit us and those we love just because we're too busy taking care of everyone else.

> We want to solve their problems, but instead, we rob them of the opportunity to learn to problem solve and the confidence that comes from being independent.

In a busy world where you're leading people, being a mommy, and building an empire, you have to find life hacks that will save you time, protect your energy, and work for *you*. There are many small (but smart) ways to start finding some extra time throughout your day so

> **Perfection stifles execution.**

that you have the time and energy to find opportunities that pay you! One example is shopping online for groceries and grabbing the food from the pick-up parking spot on your way home from the office. This just might be the thing that gives you back some time and energy.

I have found that a super greens powder mixed with peanut butter protein powder in my water has become an easy morning protein smoothie that is a healthy and quick way for me to get out the door and start my day. Working from the car while my daughter is in tutoring (so I don't waste time driving home and coming back to pick her up) is efficient and gives me an extra hour in my day. Bringing snacks or packing a lunch (instead of driving around to find a place to eat) saves me time and money.

Simplifying processes and intentionally making fewer decisions in a day will help preserve your energy for the things that matter most. Leveraging the people around you and delegating tasks to others will allow you to focus on the things that are most fulfilling and important to generating income and moving your goals forward. Believe it or not, keeping lots of balls in the air is possible if you focus on priorities and hire great people. Just because others say it's impossible, that doesn't make it impossible for you. That's their limiting beliefs coming out; that's their lid, their capacity. Make sure you know your own. Your commitment needs to be on time, blocking all things that are important to *you* and protecting your energy so you can direct it toward your priorities instead of trying to live within the boundaries set by others. The key is using your newfound time and energy in a way that is highly productive for your plan.

Another way you drain your energy and rob yourself of progress is when you have unreasonable expectations of yourself or others and an unwavering commitment to perfection. It sounds like a good thing, but perfection stifles execution! Being OK when things are imperfect will help profit and progress much more quickly. I'm not saying to release a product that lacks quality and value. Instead, I want you to understand that you have to stop somewhere and get the product to market to make a profit. You can always improve things along the way; just realize your business is a living, changing thing. You will always look to adjust and improve it. So go get some wins!

Having wins quickly will keep you energized, motivated, confident, and credible. Overthinking things and waiting until you know everything will destroy your momentum and the excitement of those around you who believe in you and are betting on you. You must run to your first wins and help your people do the same. When it's time for work, focus on the priority task at hand and move forward when it's good. When you can't let go of perfection, you lose valuable time and energy making insignificant edits that don't give you an ROI on your time or money. You could be spending that time with those you love. So just GO already!

Your physical health is another area that can impact your energy. So, if you're going to rethink how you can protect and improve yourself, consider the way you value and interact with your physical body. This will directly impact your mental health. Are you taking care of the one body you were given to get you through this life? Do you truly realize that you are shortening your opportunity to enjoy an amazing life by failing to take care of yourself physically? You're stealing from your hard work and future self because, at some point, the damage done will show up as health issues. The cost of maintaining or fixing things at that point can drain everything and everyone around you financially, physically, and emotionally.

Wouldn't it be a shame to work hard designing this life, only to find that everything you envisioned and worked so hard for would have to be sacrificed to maintain your health and that the time you had left would be spent in doctor's offices rather than traveling or doing what you absolutely love? So get real about your physical habits. You don't have to make massive changes overnight. As a matter of fact, habits will always be more sustainable and lifelong when you alter them in the right direction just 1 percent at a time.

Take a good look at your habits—eating habits, sleeping habits, exercise habits, and addictions. Are they serving you? What do you need to adjust so that your life by design is enjoyed by a healthy mind and body? Start showing up more often as the person you would like to become. Start seeing yourself as that person, and you will become exactly that. Eliminate habits that don't serve your goals, even if it's just one tiny adjustment at a time.

> Start showing up more often as the person you would like to become.

Chapter 6

PRIORITIES

Scrap your to-do list and create a *priority* list!

FOCUS ON IDENTIFYING YOUR PRIORITIES AND SIMPLIFYING a path to make them easily executable and duplicatable. Too often, we overcomplicate and overthink things to justify our inaction. So, being clear about your priorities and the steps that will get you to your goal, as well as recognizing the things that don't really matter to the mission, are key. My grandmother told me years ago that she left her house messy at times because time with her kids was more important than a clean house. So make time for the adventures, be present in the moments, make the memories, and take the trips. Life is shorter than you think, so sometimes, that requires saying no to the housekeeping for the day or even dropping something off the list that doesn't matter. Get over your perfectionism and give yourself grace in this busy world. Make your to-do list a priority list! Kick 80 percent of the "should dos" to the bottom and delegate or drop as many of those as possible. Focus on the 20 percent that are "must dos" and vital to the mission.

Give yourself permission to occasionally do the things you would never think of doing. No one will die if you serve Fruity Pebbles for dinner one night because you don't feel like cooking, and the kids would love it. And things will be just fine if the house stays a mess while you cuddle and watch movies on the couch! The only way the memories can be abundant is if you say no to things that don't matter at the moment to make time for those that do. Give yourself grace for not looking like the perfect mom on that show you watch. I promise your kids will remember the ice cream-before-dinner nights and the little impromptu adventures their whole lives. They won't remember if the house looked good that week or if the details were perfect. Hire a college student to come by and help every few weeks if necessary. They can be inexpensive and provide valuable help as you navigate your busy life. I once heard it said that the best way to find your purpose and priorities is to sit down and write your eulogy. I'm sure having a spotless house isn't the title you strive for.

The key to being OK with allowing things to drop is to sit back and reflect on what *actually* matters **(REFER TO THE GETTING CLEAR RESOURCE AT THE END OF THE CHAPTER).** What do you want your family to remember about you when you're gone? What memories do you want to make? What pastime from your childhood do you cherish the most and want to recreate? What would healthy finances and an abundant life do to help you with that? Why do you feel so strongly about building wealth? Do you have kids you'd love to see travel and go to college? Do you have a business you want to start or a charity you'd like to impact? Do you have parents who will need to be cared for when they're older? (Did you know the last few years of a person's life are the equivalent of the cost of an entire decade of their younger years?) How about a retirement vision; that's going to cost you! By saying no to things that are not priorities, giving yourself the grace to drop others, and creating a simple, executable plan, you will get there! Remember, life is a journey, not a destination, so you want to enjoy the ride!

Get *super* clear on who loses if you don't win and who wins if you do! It's often the people you love most. So make it visual! You may laugh at the idea of vision boards, but they're a genius way to keep priorities in front of your face. What you focus on, you attract. Your vision board will remind you to get back up when it's hard while helping you focus on where you're going and how much you and your family will love it. It will keep you from having to go back and start over if the vision and reflection become clouded when life gets busy. It will keep you from forgetting *why*. So make it highly visual and tie it to your pain and pleasure so that when it's hard and you want to quit, you won't! Have friends in your corner who know your goals. Speak them out loud so you have accountability. Don't be afraid of what others will

> Get super clear on who loses if you don't win and who wins if you do!

think if you fail; be afraid of where you'll still be if you never try!

The world needs you to step up and be the best version of yourself, sharing the gifts God gave you. You become magnetic when you step into your purpose and focus on becoming your best self! Key relationships find you, money finds you, opportunity finds you, and the list goes on. You have a responsibility and an obligation to become the person God knows you can be. Fulfilling your purpose on this earth is contingent on it.

> You become magnetic when you step into your purpose and focus on becoming your best self!

Getting CLEAR

1) What's the big picture for your life, and how does the hard work you're willing to put in fit into that picture?

2) Why does this vision matter so much to you? What's the story behind it that lights a fire in you?

3) Can you remember a moment when you first got excited about this vision? What made it so special?

4) What are the things that really drive you, the stuff you deeply believe in? How does the hard work you're willing to do reflect those beliefs?

5) Think back to how you developed these values. What experiences shaped them?

6) Tell about a time when you acted in line with these values. How did it make you feel?

Getting CLEAR

7.) Can you pinpoint the skills, interests, or passions that make the hard work feel like a meaningful journey?

8.) How did you discover and nurture these strengths and interests along the way?

9.) Share a story about a time when you used these strengths or followed a passion to overcome a challenge or reach a goal.

10.) What gets you pumped up about the potential rewards or results of your hard work, personal growth, success, or impact on others?

11.) Can you describe the specific goals or markers of success that get you excited?

12.) Recall a time when the idea of these rewards motivated you to push through tough times. What happened as a result?

Getting CLEAR

13.) Are there any people or experiences from your past that inspire you and remind you why hard work matters in achieving your goals?

14.) Think about someone you look up to or a past experience that left a lasting impression on your work ethic. Share a story or lesson from one of these role models or experiences that still resonates with you today.

Chapter 7

TALENT AND JOY

Identify your unique *talents.*

BELIEVE IT OR NOT, SOME PEOPLE ACTUALLY love what they do! When you identify something that feels like play to you but work to others, you've identified something that can add value to others and generate income for you. You've identified your talents, but what are those talents? Sometimes, we don't even see them in ourselves. Sometimes, we have to ask others to help identify them. I encourage you to take a pen to paper and sit in the sunshine. Put on some calm, wordless music and reflect; think about some things you have always loved.

As I reflected, I remembered that as a kid, I loved ceramics. I loved to sing and dance any chance I got. I loved to be in nature (it's where I have always felt closest to God). I also realized that most of the things that had brought me joy were no longer a part of my busy life. Perhaps that was robbing me of my joy and leaving me feeling unfulfilled. Perhaps it was robbing me of my ability to think creatively and generate valuable ideas. Perhaps it was robbing me of my desire to look for opportunities that would add value and generate income.

As I continued to reflect, I realized that I have always loved psychology as well as helping others win and solve problems. I found that when you take the time to think about solving problems for others, you often find opportunities that pay very well and generate income that can be multiplied. As you begin to think about problems you can solve for others, please remember two important facts: solving problems others can solve for themselves is called enabling, while solving problems that impact many

> Solving problems others can solve for themselves is called enabling, while solving problems that impact many and seem unsolvable is called opportunity.

and seem unsolvable is called opportunity. Make sure you're clear on the difference.

What have others told you you were good at? This can be a hard one, as we often retain the negative input and not the positive. To help me answer this question, I wrote a simple message to several people who had known me all my life and asked them, "What are some things that stand out in your mind about me? What did I love to do? How would you describe me?" I wanted the perspective of the people who knew me as an innocent child. Some I hadn't spoken to in years, but they knew me before I became the person the world told me I should be. As I went through this exercise, I noted things and people that gave me energy and the times in life when I felt my best, both mentally and physically. This was an awesome activity that helped me to identify what brings me joy and what gifts I was given.

As you reflect on the people and things that bring you joy, take some time to just freewrite with no judgment. No grammar. Just brain dump. Once you have a good list, ask yourself how you can add more of these things to your calendar. Is there a way to integrate them into the role you have now? How can you model a better life for your kids and those around you? How can you teach them to integrate joy and their God-given talents into their lives? How can these things generate income so there is more joy and money to invest?

In my life, this looks like more music, more outdoor adventures, and more think time. It looks like learning time, relationship time, and time helping people build wealth so they can bless others. It means flipping homes as a family project and helping my husband do what he loves. It means listening to podcasts on compound interest with my son in the car because being a "sneaky" parent who dumps valuable information into my child makes me happy. It means serving others with my daughter by giving what we have worked hard to earn while she watches. It means finding opportunities that will build our family vision while giving everyone a role they love. It means blasting the music and dancing together while making progress on the projects. It means taking breaks to go camping, having great conversations about what they're learning, and listening as they teach their peers.

It doesn't mean saying *yes* to everything! Instead, it means saying *no* to almost everything so we can say yes to the life *we* choose! It means we don't attend every birthday party or say yes to every invitation. It means we don't buy what others buy just to have comparable things because our financial plans for the future are different from theirs. It means saying no to what others say yes to so that we can have what others don't have—time together, with adventures included—because that is our life by design! Remember, you must prioritize your desires because, while you can have anything, you can't have everything.

> **It means saying no to almost everything so we can say yes to the life we choose!**

Please don't mishear me. When I say we don't accept all invitations, I mean that we say no to many things so we have the time, energy, and money to say yes to the things we absolutely love. We love being together as a family. We love exploring. We love being outdoors and being with our tight tribe of friends. We love learning, building, and creating. We love investing and constructing ideas into business ventures. We love treasure-hunting opportunities that will build passive income and fund our future adventures and experiences. If we said yes to all the things others would like to add to our calendar, our progress would be slow and messy rather than purposeful and progressive.

Some of the hardest noes are those that would put you on a great track to win in a single area of life. They're disguised as beneficial but at the sacrifice of a well-balanced life. Is it so important to win in one area that you lose sight of all the others? This is a question that only you can answer. It starts with getting clear on who you are and what you love while believing you are capable and worthy of having it. Understand that you don't have to fit in everywhere or be a part of everything because that actually eats at your finite resources of time, energy, and money. Don't let the words of others or your past beliefs stop you from living your purpose. Instead, ask yourself: What are my talents? What brings me joy? How can I monetize it?

> **While you can have anything, you can't have everything.**

Chapter 8

INCREASE INCOME

Turn talent into additional *income*.

IT'S NOT ABOUT AN OBSESSION WITH MONEY:
IT'S ABOUT AN OBSESSION WITH FREEDOM!

"However unpleasant those broke years were, I was motivated to go forward and depend upon myself. The war saved us. I graduated from high school with my older sister. We both got jobs at General Electric Engineering Lab in Schenectady. My mother got a job, her first. I saved every penny because I had to get a college education. Luckily, New York State Teachers College in Albany was almost free. They only accepted kids with 90 percent or over New York State Regents' averages in college entrance courses. I had that."

"School was a challenge. I lived at home, commuted by bus, and worked several jobs. The school cafeteria paid twenty-five cents per hour but gave free food. I did a semester as a babysitter, working twenty-six hours a week for room and board. I clicked nights at a Montgomery Ward. At graduation in 1948, I had half of my master's degree work done and a job teaching with my best friend at New York's Central High School in Stratford. Imagine $2,900 per year plus room and a teacherage. Katy and I were ecstatic. I taught social sciences in six different classes per day, from American history to world history. Plus, we tutored two tuberculosis patients two evenings a week. I also trained cheerleaders, and we were required to accompany the kids on school *trips to athletic events, as they invited all of the kids and wanted us to prevent 'sexual manifestation.' For the first two months, I threw up every morning and memorized my class lectures. Money was no problem. I got my teeth fixed. My family was fine. So I set out to see the world."*

—Grandma Clare

WHEN YOU CAN MONETIZE WHAT BRINGS YOU joy, you have truly created something special. Just be sure to monetize *and* scale. For instance, if you find joy in card making, make simple cards you can create in bulk. Use them to nurture your business's raving fans so they feel loved and are eager to do business with you more often. Simplify and systematize the process so it's scalable and can be duplicated by staff and systems in the future, making it financially lucrative. You don't want to create a plan that is too hard to sustain, yet you want to incorporate the things you do well and the things you love in a way that generates both joy and revenue. Success is simple, but we often overcomplicate it to justify our inaction; that's not the first or last time you'll hear me say that in this book. (I'm grateful for the quotes dropped on me over and over by my mentors!) The point? Don't overcomplicate it, or you'll create chicken exits (great excuses) and never take action. This is where most visions go to die.

> Success is simple, but we often overcomplicate it to justify our inaction.

So, if your joy is teaching, consider using recorded classes or video conferencing to teach larger audiences. If you love ceramics and making coffee mugs or funny T-shirts that draw attention to your brand, systematize making them for promotional swag or client gifts. If your joy comes from cooking, find a way to cook for more people. You may want to consider adding the skill sets you love to your current role or partnering with an existing business where your joys are leveraged, but keep in mind that you may have to drop something to add something you love. However you decide to move forward, remember that systems and processes turn ideas and talents into scalable, financially sound businesses.

When you're passionate about something, you'll do it more consistently over time. Consistency builds results like compound interest. The point of identifying what brings you joy and finding a way to monetize it is that it increases your happiness *and* your income. When you maximize income in a way that brings you joy, you will be motivated to continue for the long term and make far more money than if you were simply working a side job to earn wages and pay off debt. And you'll love showing up to work! So, if you're able to find a way to earn more in your current role or find a side hustle that brings you both joy and income, do it! Just be sure your side income doesn't become a distraction from your primary income. Build a real business and focus on it.

> Be sure your side income doesn't become a distraction from your primary income.

All too often, I see people looking for a shortcut or a magic pill. There are no get-rich-quick tricks, just tricks to get *them* rich as they attempt to sell you their plan. This is so prevalent in the wealth-building and coaching space. People go broke buying into a shortcut because they fear the actual work or the time it will take. They buy into every side hustle sold to them, and rather than increasing their income, they lose income by being distracted and focused on too many things. Nothing gets done well when you fool yourself into believing you can multitask at a high level. Focus on your highest-dollar-producing activities first and make them nonnegotiable.

Chapter 9

PASSION

***Passion* ignites productivity.**

I'VE ALWAYS HAD A LOVE FOR REAL estate because I believe homes provide security to families. They are places to rest and enjoy friends and family, and they serve as treasure boxes that hold our most precious memories. They are where our babies are raised, our biggest investments are made, and our growth happens. They appreciate in value and, with little effort, grow the net worth of families. They provide opportunities to pay for college and are where we run our home-based businesses.

Many teachers in the investment space claim that your home is *not* an investment. I hate that comment because, even though it may be a liability for you right now (by definition), it doesn't have to be and won't be forever. There are many ways to generate income with your home. As a twenty-year-old kid, the bedrooms in my brand-new build housed roommates and generated income. My brother chose to buy a home with multiple structures that rent as cabins for adventuring guests. My father rents the land around his home for weddings, business mixers, and private parties. My grandmother has a guest house that serves as a short-term rental.

There are a seemingly unlimited number of income-producing possibilities, including boarding pets, storing RVs, renting your pool, leasing your garage, renting your home seasonally for local events or retreats, leasing land for gardens, and on and on. Generating passive income with what you already have is as simple as making a decision to do so. By looking at things you currently have access to and realizing you're already more blessed than others, you will find opportunities to share, provide, rent, and leverage those assets, talents, and spaces to generate revenue. Focus primarily on passive income ideas so you're not just taking on another job that requires more time and money.

> Focus primarily on passive income ideas so you're not just taking on another job that requires more time and money.

When I first started out, real estate was a side hustle while I worked as a teacher, making almost nothing. I understood that building a portfolio of real estate investments would generate passive income and eventually free me from the need to earn income **(REFER TO THE THREE STEPS TO FREEDOM RESOURCE AT THE END OF THE CHAPTER).** I was willing to put in the hours because I believed in the impact investing had on families. It brought me joy and served my values and my mission, so I was motivated to continue, even when it was hard. (To this day, it rarely feels like work to me.) It quickly became my highest-dollar-producing activity and was soon a full-time career that financially blessed my family and many others. Over the years, it has become a strategy for building our life by design while creating opportunities for our family, friends, and many others. It has become the vehicle that funds the dreams we talk about and imagine as a family—the dreams that make the family a cohesive team on a path to an abundant and exciting future full of amazing experiences along the way.

Remember, life is an adventure, not a point of arrival, and it's not all about you. It's not just about where you're headed but who you are becoming along the way. It's a slow road but a rewarding one. The journey doesn't happen without roadblocks and detours; growth doesn't happen without struggle. It takes time and reflection and is filled with constant adjustments as you grow and change. Embrace it; don't fight it. It's your masterpiece, and you're the artist. Paint it in a way you will love and soak it up, the good and the bad. It's what reflects how uniquely made you are—the human only you can be.

3 STEPS TO
Freedom

1

YOUR JOB
PROVIDES FOR
YOU

2

YOUR JOB BUYS ASSETS THAT
HELP PROVIDE FOR YOU

3

YOUR ASSETS
PROVIDE FOR YOU

Chapter 10

SOLVE OR SERVE

Money shows up when you *solve* a problem or *serve* a need.

*PROFIT IS MADE WHEN YOU IDENTIFY
WHAT YOU HAVE AVAILABLE THAT OTHERS
COULD BENEFIT FROM AND MONETIZE IT!*

"Until I was ten years old, money was not an issue. I knew my mother's family was 'well-to-do,' and we had some inheritances. But there were a series of disasters from which our family suffered. My older sister, Geraldine, was hit by a car and hovered between life and death in Albany Hospital. My mother had my baby brother, Wilcox, and my father lost his job. This time, the inheritances had run out. We went on welfare and moved to a slum apartment in Troy, New York. My older sister was in and out of hospitals, and my mother was lost. She didn't know how to live in a place infested with bedbugs. We had bicycles. The kids in our slum area did not. I went into business renting bicycles by the hour. The price was twenty-five cents per hour, and I was really nasty about late fees and overtime. The money went to bus fare to find a place in a better area that had no bedbugs that my mother would accept and welfare would pay for. We moved into a basement apartment in Landenberg."

—Grandma Clare

WHEN THINKING ABOUT WAYS TO INCREASE INCOME, consider that people tend to move away from pain and toward pleasure. Building wealth comes by solving problems for others or by creating pleasure systematically in a scalable way over and over again.

> Building wealth comes by solving problems for others or by creating pleasure systematically in a scalable way over and over again.

When pleasure increases or pain is reduced, demand becomes high, as does opportunity for income. If you can identify a way to solve a painful problem or create pleasure for others, you can sell it. Take out a pen and brainstorm some problems you can solve in the short term with the skill set and relationships you currently have available to you. Ask yourself what the people around you need help with or access to.

This question reminds me of a need that an investor friend and I identified in our local housing market. We were running out of "affordable" housing. Developers had put "site-built only" rules on the majority of the neighboring lots, and the average consumer couldn't afford site-built homes. The housing demand had driven prices through the roof. I searched and searched for land where we could build cheaper manufactured housing, only to find that the options were almost zero. I recognized that if I could find or make this land appear, the demand would be high, income would be made, and the community would be served. So I went on a hunt and remembered something I had learned from my grandmother: If regulations are recorded on a piece of land but none of the land has been sold, those regulations can be removed. And that's just what I found—thirty-five acres with sitebuilt regulations. The listing agent could have identified the same opportunity in a heartbeat had he taken the time to think about what was available to him and the needs of the community.

The financial investment of buying that much land was out of my comfort zone at the time. So, after identifying a profitable plan, I looked at my relationships and asked myself who would see this vision and be able to afford it. I reached out and shared the vision, and sure enough, the numbers made amazing sense. Partner One was soon on board, but he was also not in a place to fund such an expensive project. So he looked at his relationships and found partners two and three. Needless to say, the three of them were thrilled at the profits produced from the idea. I traded brains and sweat equity running the project in exchange for one-fifth of the project and commissions on the sales. That project netted me more than I would have made working fifty hours a week for a year—for three years in a row! I was zero dollars in and great profits out!

I have employed this strategy several times over the years, and you can too! When you trade your knowledge and sweat equity for opportunity, it will change your life with no financial investment! There is no out-of-pocket cost, just hard work and time. You see, when you have an idea that solves a problem and can identify the right "who" in your circle of friends, you help your friends win, and you win as well. It's rewarding. It's lucrative. It's fun. And best of all, it's duplicatable.

Chapter 11

"WHO" MATTERS

Who you're in business with *matters*.

AS YOU MOVE TOWARD YOUR LIFE BY design, others will see you winning, and opportunities will start to knock. A door opened to a promising
opportunity can be exciting, but be careful. Don't get so excited about the
opportunity that you choose the wrong "who!" It's better to pass up an
opportunity, go at it alone, or say no altogether than to get into business
with the wrong people. If you move too quickly when deciding to partner
with others, even with the best intentions, the result can be a train wreck.
Trust me, I have had a few of my own!

Money should never be the obstacle to an idea that truly serves a need.
When you identify the problem you can solve and the potential for income
becomes obvious, people will come out of the woodwork to fund the idea.
I used to ask myself, "But how? I don't have the funds." I realized that if you
can communicate the vision and show that
the numbers make sense and the risk is reasonable, you don't need your own money to
create income and make a profit; the money
will always show up!

> If you can communicate the vision and show that the numbers make sense and the risk is reasonable, you don't need your own money to create income and make a profit; the money will always show up!

When it does, make sure you don't just
accept the first partnership offer. Slow
down on this part of the equation and ask
yourself some questions:

- Can I see myself winning with this person?
- Do I like them?
- Do we have matching values?
- Do they have a complementary talent to offer?
- Will we get better results together?

I can't stress enough how important this is when converting your idea into a lucrative business opportunity. I've lost hundreds of thousands of dollars by not doing my research and getting into business with people who were not the right fit just because the opportunity was exciting. This can tie you up in lawsuits for years, create huge, messy situations, and even kill friendships. So take your time and ask an outside, trusted friend who's been in partnerships before to take a look at your plan and give you honest feedback. Interview past and present relationships your potential partners have had. Find the good, bad, and ugly and determine if you are willing to deal with them at their worst. Make sure you're able to commit to the people and the project for years to come.

Don't get caught up thinking you will miss the opportunity. The truth is that opportunity arises all the time, and getting caught in the wrong one will rob you of the ability to say yes to others who may be a better fit. Ask yourself, "What more do I need to know to make this decision?" Generally, the larger the investment and profitability, the more interested potential partners, and the larger the risk and reward.

Do this part right! Take your time. Choose a business partner like you would choose a life partner. If they're the right fit, you can win together over and over again for years to come. How great is that? But if they're the wrong fit, they could cost you the right partner and hold you back from your goals for years to come.

There are several other questions you should ask yourself before saying yes to an opportunity:

- Is the profit from this project worth the time and energy it will take me to make it work?
- Is it in alignment with my future goals?
- Do I have the time, energy, and resources to be all in?

Remember, when you say *yes* to something, you will have to say *no* to several other things. Time, money, and energy are often limited resources, so you have to make sure the things you give a yes to are in alignment with your mission. Make sure your yes is something you can be excited about and committed to. When you get this right, the results can be huge, and the satisfaction is through the roof.

When you complete that lucrative project with those amazing partners, you will feel great and get to ask, "What's the next opportunity?" or "How or where can we do it again?" There's no shortcut for hard work and showing up consistently, but money, passion, and relationships can align over and over again, resulting in truly winning for your life, your family, your goals, and your philanthropy.

On a side note, if you want to test business relationships for larger projects or just contribute to something you may not want to be in for the long haul, you can find smaller problems to solve that are lucrative and have shorter timelines. These can be projects that get you in and out quickly when project opportunities look great, but long-haul project partners are still in question. They can also serve as stepping stones and provide learning opportunities that lead you to larger long-term projects with your newly tested relationships. The smaller projects take less time and money, and if you choose the wrong partners, you can generally recover with less pain. The monetary investment and reward are less, but so is the risk. Don't be afraid to start a little smaller.

Chapter 12

TAX DEDUCTIBLE

Build a business where happiness is *tax deductible*.

AS YOU WORK TO DISCOVER YOUR TALENTS and how to monetize them, consider creating a business or becoming an independent contractor in someone else's business using those talents. Owning a business can give you amazing financial benefits that being an employee cannot.

In my opinion, everyone should have a real estate license. This license allows you to build a sales or referral business. Real estate sales pay great, but if you hate selling, you never have to with a referral business. Starting a business can make you an independent contractor for tax purposes, allowing you to keep your money in your pocket by leveraging the tax benefits of the self-employed.

The average American household will pay out almost two million dollars in taxes over its lifetime! So, consider learning how to keep what you can. Having a real estate license gives you the opportunity to make passive income by simply talking to those you love, listening for life changes, and then connecting them to a great agent. You're literally paid well and get several tax benefits just by introducing people! This works for anyone you know who may need to buy or sell real estate anywhere in the world. You don't even have to "do the work" of a real estate agent. You just have to know how to find one to send your friends to.

Real estate is just one example of a business where you can be an independent contractor. I use it because I believe in it. It has a low financial barrier for entry, and it doesn't take long to get licensed. Let's discuss some of those tax deductions and how they can contribute to you living a life by design.

You don't separate life from business when you do what you love!

I always go back to adventures; I'm an experience junky! I've always loved to travel and experience different cultures and foods while meeting amazing people and enjoying the beautiful scenery God gifted us. The history of other countries and their people has always interested me. I love a good picnic at the beach or a stroll down a historic city street. I love a road trip through the mountains to take pictures of wildlife. I love looking at the architecture of historic and modern buildings. Some people spend their lives chasing happiness and never catching it. I believe that your days should incorporate the things that make you happy. Remember, it's about enjoying the journey. Happiness is a day-to-day state of mind, not something you eventually acquire.

When I was a kid, my grandmother taught me that joy comes through experiences, and most experiences can be tax deductions. Even better, if you're in business with family, you can take family adventures and make them deductible, too! Study or network with businesses in places you want to go. My family just enjoyed a ten-day road trip, seeing some of the most beautiful country while exploring the prospect of buying a campground as an investment. The time together, the sights, the people, the excursions, and the memories were all priceless and legitimately part of business research. As your income grows, consider saving it and investing it in locations you love to visit. You can buy properties in amazing destinations and share them with those you love while also renting them as short-term rentals that pay for themselves. Create experiences and memories that last a lifetime while creating a portfolio of assets that increase your net worth and passive cash flow. Even visiting them can be deductible!

Consider making time on your trips to meet new business referral partners or mentors or contribute to others' businesses by speaking or traveling to places you have always wanted to see. Look for investment opportunities as you travel. Meals and even some entertainment on the trip can be deductible if they pass the litmus test of ordinary and likely to transact. The possibilities are endless.

Always get advice from your CPA, but I can tell you that many of my favorite childhood adventures were experienced on the backs of business travel trips.

We visited real estate offices in Hawaii and Paris. We traded houses for the summer with families from other countries to make travel more affordable. We had adventures several times a year at a tiny vacation rental in Mexico that gifted our family and friends with incredible memories.

> Many of my favorite childhood adventures were experienced on the backs of business travel trips.

Traveling to teach others or to learn more about business and leadership has become one of my favorite ways to adventure. Joining a company that coached and taught near sandy beaches provided fun opportunities for my family to jump in on some beach time and stay at nice hotels. They would swim and play while I had my meetings, and we would end our days with our toes in the sand after a delicious dinner—all tax deductible! If you change your mindset from "I have to" to "I get to," you will fall in love with this work and life mix. Ask yourself what's the next best thing you can do *today* to start making this a reality.

Make a game of integrating your business into everything you do. When you become a business owner, cars become deductions, gas mileage becomes deductible, and even a portion of your home and utilities can become deductible if you have space for a home office. As I mentioned earlier, taxes are one of the biggest expenses you'll pay in your lifetime, so you should really consider finding a side hustle where you are self-employed and get the incredible deductions available to you as a business owner. The purpose of the tax code is to flow money through the economy the way the government sees fit, and it allows many great ways to reduce your taxable income if you do so.

> The purpose of the tax code is to flow money through the economy the way the government sees fit, and it allows many great ways to reduce your taxable income if you do so.

Legally reducing your taxes is fun, and this alone will allow you to keep much more of your hard-earned money in your pocket. Your side hustle may become the full-time hustle that funds your life by design, just like mine did.

Full disclosure: I am *not* a tax professional, so find a great one and educate yourself about taxes. Don't be afraid to fire them and move on if they're unwilling to think outside the box. There are benefits for businesses that create new jobs, affordable housing, educational opportunities, and the like. Still, most tax accountants are so focused on not getting audited that they fail to accept that the tax code is written to encourage businesses to flow money through the economy. The tax code is extensive and changes often, so it takes effort to keep up with the ins and outs of how it works. By understanding the tax code, you actually get to help the economy and, in turn, help yourself by keeping more of your hard-earned money.

My grandmother would always book trips around places where she was interested in investing in real estate. This would allow her to tour the area, take a continuing education class, stop in a brokerage to educate herself about the opportunities it had to offer, and create referral partners with the local agents. Remember when I told you to go get a real estate license? There is a method to my madness!

In the last two years, I have enjoyed some of my greatest adventures that were also tax deductible. Finding training with high-level individuals who are learning about business and life in some of the most beautiful areas in the country has resulted in amazing adventures for my family and me. I have built some lifelong friendships and enjoyed many hours in the sun watching the sailboats and enjoying delicious dinners, all in the name of education. To make it even better, I have found friends and family who I love to adventure with, and they have joined me for the same training. Now, as we better our lives, we get to travel and enjoy time together, all tax deductible.

Not only are there tax benefits, but travel and education can be a blast when your children and friends are a part of it. If you pay for that education, it's also a deduction and may save you huge amounts of money in taxes while building skills over time. I can't stress this enough. Go jump into one of my favorite books, *Tax-Free Wealth*, by Tom Wheelwright. No doubt you will see things differently and come out with more money to invest in your future. Become a student of wealth and make it fun!

Consider employing your friends and family if they're a good fit for the position. Look into the tax benefits of employing your kids and giving them job skills at an early age.

That money you want to set aside

> **Look into the tax benefits of employing your kids and giving them job skills at an early age.**

for your child's future can become deductible when they're working in your business. You're contributing to a retirement account for them. The money you pay them stays in the family and is taxed at a lower tax bracket because they don't make much income. It also teaches them valuable life skills. I'd encourage you to educate yourself on this topic.

Giving to your favorite charity, helping a child through private school, and even doing business with people who know you, love you, and trust you are blessings that can easily turn into enjoyable lunches together and opportunities to grow and benefit one another. Even gifts become deductible. Recently, I went to the mailbox and found a check for $5,000 that was written to send my kids to private school. It was sent by someone I had barely met, who, over the years, has continued to find ways to bless us while impacting her bottom line. Because of her financial habits, she now has the ability to change lives and is fulfilled when she does so. It's deductible to her and a blessing to us.

> Because of her financial habits, she now has the ability to change lives and is fulfilled when she does so.

Every time I see her doing these kinds of things, I am reminded of how preparing yourself financially not only changes lives but changes people. I will forever be a different human because I am completely moved and humbled by her generosity, which has blessed and changed my family. When you truly slow down and look around, you will find raving fans silently cheering you on, and you owe it to them to show up strong and do the work. Go win! You owe it to your family, yourself, and God, who blessed you with the ability to do so.

If wealth creates freedom, and freedom is the ability to do what you want, when you want, and with whom you want, then it's not greedy or selfish to build wealth. You're simply using it as a tool to live life on your terms and bless those you love. It provides priceless experiences to others. It gifts opportunities that change the lives of those you love. It creates jobs, builds businesses, solves problems, provides healthcare, gifts experiences, and allows you to give generously. Why don't we do a reality check and find out where you are now? Where do you want to go? How do you start today with the Net Worth Tracking worksheet (**REFER TO THE NET WORTH**

It creates jobs, builds businesses, solves problems, provides healthcare, gifts experiences, and allows you to give generously.

TRACKING RESOURCE AT THE END OF THIS CHAPTER). Without knowing where you are and what your income and expenses *really* look like, how could you ever create a plan to build abundance and live your life by design?

NET WORTH CALCULATOR

Scan for a wealth tool that calculates your Net Worth in real time!

Net Worth Calculator

Name: [Name]   As of: [date]

Net 1 Million

Goal ■ $

Assets		
Cash		
Checking accounts	116,000	1000000
Savings accounts	119,000	
CDs (certificates of deposit)		
Life Insurance (cash value)		
Other cash	25,000	
Total Cash	260,000	
Investments		
Securities (stocks, bonds, mutual funds)	155,000	
Treasury Bills		
Other investments		
Total Investments	155,000	750000
Property		
Real Estate (market value)	1,253,000	
Automobile (present value)	4,000	
Bullion (silver, gold, etc)		
Jewelry, Art and Collectibles		
Other property		
Total Property	1,257,000	
Retirement		
Retirements accounts (IRA, 401k)		
Employer Pensions ($/month * 240)		500000
Social Security ($/month * 240)		
Other assets		
Total Retirement	-	
Notes and Accounts receivable		
Total Assets	**1,672,000**	

Liabilities		
Accounts Payable		
Auto Loan	22,000	250000
Credit Card Debt		
Consumer Loans or Installments		
Loan on Life Insurance		
Personal Home Mortgage	130,000	
Other Real Estate Mortgages	590,000	
Student Loans	20,000	
Unpaid Taxes		
Money Owed to Others		
Other liabilities		
Total Liabilities	**762,000**	0
Net Worth	**910,000**	

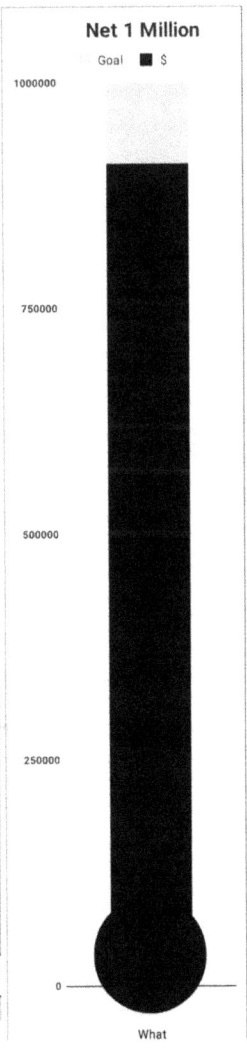

What

Chapter 13

MONEY MANAGER

Make sure your *money* is working for you and toward your life by *design*.

AFTER ALL, THE WORD DESIGN IN ITSELF means created with a plan. I encourage you to have a date with your money at least once per month to hold your money accountable (**REFER TO THE MONEY DATE RESOURCE AT THE END OF THE CHAPTER**). Make sure it's working for you and doing what you want it to do. Ask your money the following questions monthly:

> Have a date with your money at least once per month to hold your money accountable.

- How much money came in, and how did I make it?
- How much money went out, and how did I spend it?
- What spending was unnecessary?
- Did I transfer money to my savings?
- Did I pay myself first? (We will dive into this a little later.)
- Did my money grow in the vehicle it's in?
- How can I make my money work at least 1 percent better next month?
- What's the next step I am moving toward in my financial plan?
- Did I intentionally learn more about wealth building this month?
- Am I speaking my goals to someone further ahead on this journey?

Not long ago, I was asked by one of my mentors to start tracking my net worth because if you know where you are and where you're going, you can get there faster. Once you are aware of what goes in and how it drains out, you can identify what holes to patch in your wealth bucket. Your spending habits are tied to the fact that you don't focus on how incredibly blessed you are. Instead, you're trying to make yourself happy with things. For the record, *things* will never make you happy; you'll just need more things!

> Get clear on how amazing your life actually is, and your need to find happiness in "things" will go away and save you a fortune.

So get clear on how amazing your life *actually* is, and your need to find happiness in "things" will go away and save you a fortune. By tracking, you can identify the habits that are not serving you. Your monthly money date will be an eye-opener. I know mine was! Money was pouring from the bottom of my savings bucket in the form of techy tools and eating out. Once I identified my survival expenses and my acceptable, optional expenses, I was able to put some easy money hacks in place to ensure I was not slowly losing while thinking I was winning. I had to block my chicken exits. I knew what excuses I'd make to keep those tools and restaurant food. I am the queen of justifying purchases I don't need! I was floored by the results after just a single year. It's true when they say we often underestimate what we can do in a year, and compounded over several, the results can be exponential.

Start by asking yourself what your average monthly income is. If you have multiple sources, make sure you account for all of them. If you don't have multiple sources, ask yourself how you can increase your current income. How can you do more with what you are already doing? How can you spend less to increase your net profit? And finally, what other income streams could be added?

When I consider adding income streams, I always ask myself a number of questions:

- What do I truly have time for?
- What can I say no to that will make the time available?
- What am I willing to commit to?
- What will I enjoy that doesn't take a lot of extra time and effort?

I won't know the answers to some of these questions until I have a date with my money. I call these appointments my Red Light, Green Light "money dates" **(REFER TO THE RED LIGHT, GREEN LIGHT WORK-SHEET AT THE END OF THE CHAPTER).** Let's get started learning about your habits and building your life by design!

Initially, gathering the necessary information will require a commitment and time. Although it may take a bit of effort to put the following list together and plug it into the net worth tracker, once it's in, it's a simple thirty-minute maintenance, and you will love watching your net worth grow.

Gather three months worth of the following:

- Most Recent Account Balances
    - checking accounts
    - savings accounts
    - credit card accounts
    - retirement accounts
    - stocks/bonds/mutual funds
    - cash-value life insurance policies
    - cash on hand
- Real Estate Market Values
    - primary home
    - rental property
    - vacant land
    - commercial property
    - fractional interest in real estate investments
- Personal Asset Values
    - art collections
    - jewelry
    - automobiles
- Liabilities
    - student loan balances
    - car loan balances
    - mortgage balances
    - taxes owed
    - miscellaneous personal loans

- Business Value and Liabilities (if you have them)
  - business Assets/Equipment
  - business loan balances
  - business taxes owed

As you move through this process, keep in mind that your monthly goal will be to improve profit by at least 1 percent by increasing income and decreasing expenses. I recommend you play Red Light, Green Light monthly or, at minimum, quarterly. The key will be to play it regularly.

Once I have all the necessary information collected, I sit down on a quiet morning with two to three months' worth of bank statements from each of my accounts as well as red, green, and yellow highlighters. I look at each expense individually and ask if it's a survival expense. If my answer is yes, I ask if I am justifying it as a necessity when, in fact, it's not. I also ask whether I can find it cheaper or if it's part of another product I am already paying for. I can't tell you how often I have paid for two products that provide a similar result. Next, I ask, "Do I love it? Do I use it? Would I buy it again?"

If I can find it within another program I already have or decide not to buy it again, I highlight it in *red* to remind myself to eliminate the expense. If it's just a want and not a necessity, or if I might be able to find it cheaper, I highlight it in *yellow* so that I know to watch it, use caution, and price shop. If it's a true necessity, like power, water, or the mortgage, I highlight it in *green*.

I then go to my Expense Tracker worksheet and plug in all the green (regularly recurring) expenses, along with their due dates (**REFER TO THE EXPENSE TRACKER RESOURCE AT THE END OF THE CHAPTER**). I also tag them as manually paid or automatically paid so I know if I need to take action. This helps me calculate my worst-case scenario, need-to-survive income numbers, and the dates I need to pay attention to in order to maintain good

> Good credit is your integrity rating in the financial world; it helps you keep more money in your pocket by securing lower interest rates and helping you attract great investment partners when you're investing.

credit. Good credit is your integrity rating in the financial world; it helps you keep more money in your pocket by securing lower interest rates and helping you attract great investment partners when you're investing.

The yellows go in as "optional expenses," allowing me to know what I need to make to have the extra things I desire. This number is flexible and even cancelable if need be. The red items are the "no more" and are eliminated. They are things that are robbing my family of their investments, experiences, retirement, and future.

Before we leave the topic of expenses, I want to challenge you to switch from the old way of thinking, that is, **Income – Expenses = Profit,** and start thinking **Income – Profit (what you keep) = Expenses (what you have left to pay bills, including taxes).** This way of thinking may differ from what you learned in the past, but it will allow you to live below your means, save before you spend, and only spend from what you have left in your expense bucket. This model changes you from being a person who spends everything they make (having little left for themselves) to becoming a person who prioritizes themselves and their goals above their expenses and is mindful of where their money goes and what its job is. It allows you to recognize when you have gone over budget immediately.

You should also consider the following: If you own a business and have a role in that business, add yourself (your role) as a line item expense. This will result in you being paid as the owner (profit) *and* for your role in the business before any money is spent on other expenses. Because it is already built into the budget, this added line item will allow you to remove yourself from that role in the future and hire someone to take your place.

The next step in your money date is to list all your assets, such as stocks, retirement accounts, cash accounts (cash is not an asset but a tool to acquire them), real estate, cars, valuables, and personal property. Beside each of these, write the current value and the amount of debt you still owe; these are your liabilities. Also, note the interest rate on each debt, the due date, and the payments.

When you plug these numbers into the net worth tracker **(REFER TO THE NET WORTH TRACKER RESOURCE IN CHAPTER 12),** it will help you know where you truly stand in your finances. Your net worth tracker is a piece of your "game of life" scorecard. It doesn't just show if you're winning at earning; it also shows whether you're winning or losing at keeping what you work so hard for—what you trade your life for! It's far more important than just tracking your income and celebrating what you made. It's what sets the high earners apart from the truly wealthy. This will be the benchmark by which you measure progress toward your wealth goals. You will use it as a tool to direct your path and determine your next action steps. And though it will take an investment of a few hours on a quiet morning, it will be the foundation and measure of everything you do financially in the future. You can use these tools as live trackers forever, so getting them set up is worth the time.

The easiest way to get the information you need is to grab statements, log into online banking, or simply call their 1-800 numbers. Give yourself a deadline to get this done, and reward yourself (reasonably) when you have completed the task. Ask someone who loves you to hold you accountable and share with them why you're doing it and why it's important to your future. Choose someone who intimidates you a wee bit. Someone you don't want to let down. Someone who loves you fiercely and will call you out if you fail to prioritize your future.

I promise this exercise will change your life and the lives of those close to you if you commit to doing it! You'll be amazed at the free money you find that was yours all along! It often adds up to thousands annually! That, combined with increasing your earnings, is a good start to funding your future investment opportunities. And remember, your monthly goal should be to improve profit by at least 1 percent by increasing income and decreasing expenses. So commit to having regular dates with your money by playing Red Light, Green Light. This is non-negotiable if you want to master a life of wealth-building and financial freedom.

MONEY DATE

Lack of attention is one of the BIG reasons people fail
at the money game.
Keep a consistent, simple monthly date with your
money, and you will see it grow faster than you
imagined! Every month on the same day ask yourself:

Scan for a simple Profit & Loss tool!

	YES	NO
1. Did I maximize my income opportunities?	☐	☐
2. How much went in?	☐	☐
3. How much came out?	☐	☐
4. What spending was unnecessary?	☐	☐
5. Did I transfer to savings?	☐	☐
6. Did I pay down debt?	☐	☐
7. Did I pay myself first?	☐	☐
8. Did I give?	☐	☐
9. Did it grow in the vehicle it's in?	☐	☐
10. How can I make it work just 1% better?	☐	☐
11. What got in my way?	☐	☐

What did you learn about yourself and your patterns?

_____

_____

Redlight GREENLIGHT

Q1: Highlight survival expenses GREEN on all of your statements, then list and total below. Are there cheaper solutions to having these things?

Q2: Highlight optional or luxury expenses YELLOW on all of your statements, then list and total below. Are there cheaper solutions to having these things?

Q3: Highlight unnecessary expenses RED on all of your statements, then list and total below. Call the next business day to cancel them if they are auto pay. This is your new found money for your abundance account!

Freedom #=Green+Yellow x 12

Expense TRACKER

List your regularly occurring expenses in order of due date below.
Scan the code to get my Expense Tracker Tool in for the
spreadsheet form that auto-calculates for you!

Expense	Due	Rate	Balance
TOTAL			

Chapter 14

BE INTENTIONAL

Reverse engineer the *plan*.

YOU'VE IDENTIFIED YOUR KEY RELATIONSHIPS. You've started to see opportunities in many things. You're aware of your God-given talents. But how do you put it all together?

You're going to have to identify the key components to winning at *"your game"* and reverse engineer the plan. You will also need people with a backbone who love you fiercely to hold you accountable. Speak your goals to them in as much detail as possible. Share when and how you want them to check in on your progress. Give them permission and encourage them to hold you accountable and be direct. Share with them what winning will actually do for your life and who else this will affect if you do or don't get to the goal. If you don't have people like this in your life, hire a coach.

Then, create an environment that allows you to focus, encourages you to be creative, and pushes you to reach your goals—an environment that also has moments of discomfort because the bar is high and the people around you stretch you and believe in you. The most dangerous place you can be in life is a place of comfort. Comfortable people don't grow!

Think of the things you've identified in the earlier chapters, things you love, and things that bring you energy, like travel, teaching, or key relationships. If these things are truly important to you, they need to show up in your plan, your budget, and your calendar. A life by design is exactly that: a reflection of the things you discovered you wanted as you dug deeper, self-discovered, created a vision and devised a plan of action.

Ask yourself, "What's the one thing, if I accomplished nothing else in the next ninety days, that would move me closer to my life by design?"

"I felt trapped. Either I had to earn more money or find and marry a very rich man who would not mind supporting my family. Although I had met the love of my life, I seriously considered joining the armed services as an officer, as I could provide dependent payments and possibly housing for my dependents. Guess what? Things became more critical. We went back to Cottonwood, and I married Jack in October. I must've become pregnant on our honeymoon. At that time, teachers were not ever pregnant. Shortly after having another and having two babies in diapers, I tried to work part-time with no luck, and then I made the decision to become a realtor. I fully intended to go back to teaching at some time, but real estate enabled me to take care of kids after nursery school and grade school and my mother, who was living with us. I was willing to work weekends, and Jack loved his kids and stayed with them."

—Grandma Clare

Sometimes in life, it can feel like everything is going great, and then, suddenly, you find yourself in the washing machine on the heavy load setting. This has a lot to do with whether your approach to life is proactive or reactive. I can remember a time as a kid when my family was bound by money—or the lack of it. We were held back by the limited availability of information needed to improve our skill sets and generate more income. We fell into the jobs of our parents because it was all we knew. Back then, we couldn't afford the time or the money to learn a new trade, and the opportunity to learn whatever we wanted was much more complicated than going to YouTube or reaching out to our favorite mentor.

When we're bound by a lack of money because of low income or high debt, our time is tied up in trying to make more just to survive. Believe it or not, this often has less to do with our income and more to do with our current beliefs, mindset, lifestyle, and lack of time-blocking priorities. Money, or the lack of it, is one of the major causes of divorce. Our relationships become filled with stress, anxiety, fighting, abuse, and dissatisfaction because there is always a level of financial fear and pressure weighing on them.

> When we're bound by a lack of money because of low income or high debt, our time is tied up in trying to make more just to survive.

Our kids often end up unsupervised or in the care of others. This can place them at the mercy of outside influences while we're busy working to keep up with a lifestyle or just put food on the table. Often, our health care is pushed to the back burner or even neglected completely, and our ability to make memories and experience the true beauty of life is limited to hoping to do "that thing" someday versus actually doing it. Our ability to help those we love and bless others we have never met is a challenge, and to do so financially is almost impossible. We are simply reacting to life and trying to stay afloat. This is a perpetual cycle that can last for generations.

You must be the one to break the generational curse of bad money habits. You must fall in love with the limitless rewards of delayed gratification rather than the temporary happiness of instant gratification. The truest rewards come from being able to support the things and the people you love in their times of need. In order to have the time, energy, and funds needed to lead your children, friends,

> You must fall in love with the limitless rewards of delayed gratification rather than the temporary happiness of instant gratification.

coworkers, and peers, you must stay ahead of where they are so that you can inspire them, lift them, and show them the possibilities while adding value to their lives. None of this is accomplished in an environment of clutter, financial lack, stress, or drama. You must get your world right so you can be valuable to theirs.

The Bible says the borrower is a slave to the lender. That's never been more true than today. In politics, education, business, and life, it seems that everywhere we look, people are slaves to those who fund them. We try to shortcut the process by borrowing on credit lines and giving in to our

> Do the work required! You're not rewarded for the dreams you have or how smart you are. You're rewarded for the actions you take and your execution of the plan.

entitled "I deserve" mentalities. We have a responsibility to be an example for our littles and others we love. If we're not leading them, we should be concerned with who is.

My generation graduated from college with astronomical amounts of student loans and credit card debt that crippled their start into adulthood, all for the benefit of profiting corporations. No one will teach our kids or those important to us, like the ones who love them most. Teach them to be conscientious with their hard-earned money. Teach them that the world is full of marketing meant to benefit and profit others. Teach them that they can be an observer without being a consumer. Be the leader they need us to be so that they can become the best version of themselves.

Being able to experience the beautiful things God created in this world (and the amazing things history has left behind) with those we love is priceless. The ability to impact generations, teach, lead, and truly change lives goes well beyond monetary value. It takes sacrifice and long-term thinking. It takes intentionality, gratitude, delayed gratification, and financial discipline. It takes a *plan* and purposeful execution, but it will be worth every second! So let's get started on that plan, *your* plan to freedom!

Chapter 15

FAMILY BANK

Become the *bank* so you're not a slave to another lender.

BUILDING A BANKING SYSTEM THAT WORKS FOR you is the key to financial success. Make sure it's easy, visual, sustainable, and able to grow over time. Don't be intimidated if it looks overwhelming. It's a plan you're working toward, and plans take time on task over time. It's your road map; don't hide it in a drawer. Keep it front of mind and visit it monthly.

Our Family Banking System is built around the acronym FAMILY. It is separated into six sections that will help you recognize where you are financially, identify your needs and wants, and plan and take action toward your goals.

The six sections include:

- Foundation: identifying your basic needs
- Abundance: identifying and funding your dreams
- Moat: identifying and protecting the things that are valuable to you
- Investment: identifying your personal, long-game strategies for sustained wealth
- Liabilities/lifestyle: identifying ways to eliminate debt and minimize taxes
- Yearly income needed: identifying total annual income needed to live life by design

F-oundation

What is the minimum monthly income you *need* to survive (the green in Red Light, Green Light)? What is absolutely necessary? This includes expenses such as food, shelter, and basic (i.e., must-have) utilities. What do your optional expenses total? Adding this total to your green expenses will let you know what you need to make to cover your necessities plus the extra things you and your family use often.

A-bundance

Experiences. What trips do you want to take this year? What will they cost you? What income will be lost by taking time off work? Calculate it, research it, and determine the actual numbers. And if you can afford them, put them on your calendar and pay the deposits. I have found that I stay committed to a plan when it's on the calendar and money is down. When the final payment comes due, it's harder to cancel and easier to fund when it's already partially paid for. And there's no greater feeling than when you're on vacation, and your investments and businesses are making you money while you sleep and play. Take the time to explore ways you can tie experiences to your business and get tax benefits while enjoying those you love.

Think about it. What experiences are you and your loved ones missing because of your present budget, your lack of flexibility, or your belief that lots of money is required? Life is full of more adventure and fun when you add a little spontaneity. Don't be afraid to take a cheap last-minute trip or stay with a friend if you can't afford the full experience. You'll have a blast!

Wants. What do you want to see happen in the next five years? How about the next ten or twenty? It may be paying off your mortgage or making the down payment on a vacation home on the beach. Reverse engineer the math so that you know what it will take monthly to make it happen. You can be anywhere you want to be in just five years if you have a plan and *do* the work required! You're not rewarded for the dreams you have or how smart you are. You're rewarded for the actions you take and your execution of the plan. You don't have to be the smartest one in the room to build the most abundant life. You just have to be the best at consistently getting the priorities done.

What I love about life is that there are no real limits. The only limits are the ones you place on yourself. The real truth is that you can be, do, or have *anything* you want if you believe it's possible and build habits around the activities required to make it so. And you can literally have *anything* in life that can be bought if you find ways to make it pay for itself.

Giving. Who else needs your money? Who loses if you don't win? Is there a charity you love that needs your support? Do you want to give the gift of travel and experience to those you love? Are your parents in need of financial assistance? Do you have kids who need help with a car or will be headed to college? The ability to provide your kids with college funds versus watching them start out life in the red, with huge student debt, is one of the greatest gifts you can give.

The gift my grandmother loved giving was the opportunity for travel, experiences, and personal growth. I have many amazing memories of wild adventures with her. She once took me to Egypt following a terrorist attack that killed sixty-three tourists because flights were cheap and security was high. At that moment, I thought she was crazy, but looking back, I'm thankful she budgeted for it and took the risk.

That particular trip was a once-in-a-lifetime adventure that, in hindsight, my kids may never get to experience. The world has changed so much and has so many dangers that didn't previously exist. I had the opportunity to see mummies of ancient kings and queens and the pyramids while experiencing the region's history, a history I had only read about in books. I visited the vast Sahara desert, where I found a unique petrified seashell, affirming the story of Noah and my faith. This may sound insignificant, but it played a huge role in confirming and solidifying my beliefs. I experienced food and culture that I would have never understood had I not stepped foot there, and an unspoken understanding of other cultures and the challenges they face grew inside of me. I shared my passion and love with the children there and experienced the loneliness of being far away from my own relationships at home. My comfort was challenged, and my eyes were opened to a completely different world that was so beautiful.

Becoming the person you were created to be has so much to do with exploring the world and opening your eyes to other ideas—an open-mindedness and awareness you could never get from being stationary. My grandmother understood the gift of travel, and this particular gift grew me as a human in so many ways.

Because travel was important to her, my grandmother kept the cost low by never having her heart set on a particular place or experience. Instead, she was always willing to pivot when the deals came up. She wasn't dead set on one idea, one way of doing something, or the "right" timing. Instead, she was committed to providing adventures and educational and cultural experiences for those she loved. She found travel opportunities as they presented themselves and rolled with them.

Through my adventures with her, I learned how to squeeze dollars and make them work for me. I also learned the importance of leveraging relationships to make the gift of travel more easily accessible. She often traded houses with those she knew across the globe or bunked with distant family and friends to make the trips possible and more affordable. It increased the authenticity of the experience and introduced new relationships. The experience mattered, as did the savings, and she never turned down an adventure because it wasn't in the budget.

If you search your network, I bet you'll find people all over the world to connect with while gifting your loved ones adventures and memories along the way. Start getting to know your friends and distant family. You may find that you can collaborate on ideas and adventure together or just meet up for lunch as you travel across the country. Because my grandmother values relationships, I know cousins in Egypt, Costa Rica, and Belize and have friends all over the world.

It's been amazing to watch my brother adopt this same travel and relationship bug. He's been to more countries and had more amazing experiences on a budget than anyone I have ever met. He's worked with top fashion designers and eaten more strange food than I can list here. He has relationships across the globe that could take him anywhere and help him be or have anything his heart desires. Like my grandmother, my brother always finds a way to live life to its fullest and gift those he loves with the same opportunities, regardless of money. Isn't that the definition of true wealth?

Travel and adventure require income and free time—income saved to make travel possible and passive income flowing to pay for expenses while you're away from work. The true definition of a wealthy life is having freedom from a job while having the time and money to bless others and create experiences with those you love. The concepts in the Family Banking System will help you get there.

M-oat

Emergency Fund. A moat is something that protects the things that are valuable to you. An emergency fund is just that: a few thousand dollars tucked away in case the car breaks or you have to pay a deductible for health insurance. It doesn't have to be a lot, but it needs to be enough to keep you from using credit if an emergency occurs. And for most people, it needs to be in an out-of-sight, out-of-mind account that you won't be tempted to use. After your emergency account is fully funded, start focusing on your reserve account.

Reserves. This number is six months to a year of living expenses. Transitioning into other phases of life and even balancing our day-to-day realities can sometimes catch us off guard and take time to navigate and adjust. Having six months to a year set aside in reserves will allow you time to transition into your new lifestyle and adjust to living off your passive versus active income. It will also protect you in the event you're forced to transition because of an illness or unforeseen conditions, such as the Covid pandemic, which shut down so many jobs and businesses. As you're building your reserve account, you should also be identifying what amount of passive, monthly income will allow you to continue living an abundant life when or if the active income turns off. Most people have no real plan or designated account specifically tasked with growing passive income or building their retirement fund.

When do you plan on retiring? What does retiring mean to you? What will you need to retire comfortably? These are often questions asked by people but never answered. These questions have always frustrated me because they are usually based on how much you *save* so that you can live off your savings and posted in terms of cash in your account at age sixty-five. But if I've created a life I love, why would I retire? And I certainly don't want to live by depleting my savings! I want to live off passive income from cash-flowing assets and interest earned so I can pass it along for generations—multiplying it, not just using it up! In other words, it's less about the amount of money saved and more about the passive income being generated and the cumulative value of the assets.

> I want to live off passive income from cash-flowing assets and interest earned so I can pass it along for generations—multiplying it, not just using it up!

Let's make this simple. Find your freedom number **(A FORMULA FOR FINDING YOUR FREEDOM NUMBER, WHICH IS LOCATED AT THE BOTTOM OF THE RED LIGHT, GREEN LIGHT RESOURCE IN CHAPTER 13).** This number is the amount of passive income you need to fully satisfy your living expenses annually. Once you achieve this amount of passive income, you no longer need a full-time job. You will be living off the income from your investments while they continue to appreciate, and you will be able to fully enjoy the life given to you.

You often hear that you should have lower fixed expenses after retirement (which also means less deductions). When making this assumption, however, people often forget about unforeseen circumstances, like medical issues, long-term care, and inflation. Maximizing your passive income, lowering expenses, and having adequate insurance coverage will protect you. Think about your parents; are they covered? From the time I was young, I always knew that my parents had not been taught to have a plan, and even though they would never ask it of me, if I didn't help them build one, I was going to be "it." I constantly explored ways to keep them living below their means and strategies to build cash flow with what they did have in preparation for the future when they would be too old to work. Thank God my brain was always thinking this way because when my father was only sixty-seven years old, he had a crazy accident, layered by divorce, that left him limited in his ability to generate income. Thankfully, he had the cash flow I had set up by investing his money in a seller carry note years earlier.

You might also need to buy health care or long-term policies for your parents if their care will be your future cost. It's a good idea to investigate family health histories in case you decide to plan for specific health issues that could arise in the future. I know this is something you don't want to hear, but it could save you $100,000 a year in the future. The cost of being unprepared for surprises can rob you of everything you worked so hard to build. So don't fail to think these things through. You're welcome!

> The cost of being unprepared for surprises can rob you of everything you worked so hard to build.

In reality, the last years of your life are significantly more expensive. As a matter of fact, they can cost hundreds of thousands of dollars and drastically change your plans. Don't fall victim to reactive retirement. Don't be unprepared and let it fall on your kids. Don't end up with a crappy quality of life and poor healthcare because you have no plan. Imagine the future opportunities you're robbing of your kids if they have to work to support the most expensive years of your life.

Be honest with yourself on this. It's a real problem, and some kids end up taking care of multiple parents, significantly affecting their ability to build the future they want for themselves and their families. Often, I have seen children exhausted and financially drained while dealing with attorney fees and probate as they try to support parents in their final years or settle their estates. Don't be that parent; have a plan! If it's not cash saved, it can be cash flow from investments that you can leave to them or sell to support yourself. Maintaining this cash flow and a rental LLC will maximize deductions and allow you to keep more in your pocket for the future.

Insurance will protect you in the event of a massive medical need or long-term care that can bankrupt you, so make sure you have good advisors to guide your decisions. Use the Protect Your Assets worksheet to help you think through and develop a plan that protects your family and their assets as you grow your portfolio **(REFER TO THE PROTECT YOUR ASSETS WORKSHEET AT THE END OF THE CHAPTER)**. It may also be a useful tool when thinking through how to help your parents and loved ones protect theirs.

I-nvestment

The Family Bank Appreciating Assets Account. What you spend your money on matters! Remember how hard you worked to get it and don't just let it flow like water through a hole in your wealth bucket. If that happens, you'll feel like you never have enough because it leaves before it's ever full. I don't mean to imply that you can never enjoy the money you worked so hard for, but remember, this is a long game. Sustained wealth is built over time, and wealth that really blesses is built from intention, strategy, and patience. The key to building wealth is to buy and hold things that go up in value.

> **Whenever I spend from my wealth bucket, I always ask myself if this purchase is giving or taking from my future financial goals.**

Whenever I spend from my wealth bucket, I always ask myself if this purchase is giving or taking from my future financial goals. If you choose to use it to buy something that is not creating income, pay yourself back with interest, just like you do with a bank loan. You would pay the bank to borrow their money, so why not honor yourself and your hard work in the same way rather than just letting it flow out and disappear?

A few years ago, a friend introduced me to the infinite banking system, using life insurance. I was instantly curious, but because I wasn't familiar with the concept, I dug around, educated myself, questioned everything, and compared it against the knowledge I had acquired building wealth using real estate. It was an incredible journey that led to an aha moment that was right in front of my face! My grandmother had built a family banking system that changed our lives and blessed our family beyond our wildest dreams.

When I think back, it's amazing how much an intentional plan can grow in a few years, and it's absolutely incredible what it can become in a lifetime! We had a system that I had never thought much about **(REFER TO THE FAMILY BANKING WORKSHEET AT THE END OF THE CHAPTER).**

It funded college, travel, health, projects, weddings, business start-up ideas, and the like. Once the hard work and managing expenses created profit, that profit funded a banking system from which we could all request funding to move our lives forward.

There were rules to this fund, and it was protected and managed by members of the family who acted as a board of directors, if you will. If we wanted to fund an experience, an automobile, a depreciating asset, or similar things that would not generate income, we made a request and were generally approved for a loan with a payment schedule that included interest back to the fund. This accomplished both our goal and the fund's growth goals. If we were funding higher education, we were not required to pay it back.

If we bought income-generating assets, the income would either come back to the Family Bank or be paid back with interest, like a mortgage, serviced by the title company and secured by the real estate asset, allowing it to grow even larger. Land was often split and sold because the income produced far exceeded keeping it as a single property. Single-family homes were remodeled into multifamily units because cash flow increased with multiple tenants. Homes were fixed and flipped if the numbers made sense. Everything was done with the purpose of growing the Family Bank. In our current banking system, incoming funds are being used to pay down mortgages on assets. We don't have anyone spending for college, weddings, cars, or experiences at the moment, so our goal is to pay off the assets and increase our cash flow for retirement.

> Everything was done with the purpose of growing the family bank.

Because there were rules and checks and balances, this system made multimillionaires out of many of my family members as real estate assets were acquired, upgraded, and divided among them. Tax-advantaged strategies were used to keep the funds in the system, and jobs and businesses were created to teach the children how to generate revenue to do it all over again.

I have since put my own spin on this foundation, learned from some of the challenges faced by my extended family, and implemented a similar system in my own family. The neatest part is that it started from zero and grew to financial freedom and generational blessings in as little as eight years! So, how many years do you have before retirement? What can you contribute annually? You can do this!

Do you have an investment idea or project that needs capital? How much? What can you afford to put aside for it? Where can you cut to create more money to set aside? Automate that deposit to your Family Bank until you can fund the project that multiplies the money. If you don't have a specific project now, you will still want cash for future projects, so start adding. If opportunities arise that bring profit, you want to be able to act. When you consider spending from this bucket, ask yourself if your purchase will have a financial return. Ideally, you only spend this money on things that will make you money! This can start small and build into a down payment on a rental, which can then become a portfolio of cash-flowing investments. Eventually, it can be an account that funds such things as college, travel, health, businesses, projects, and weddings, becoming your own personal bank or a bank for others that generates interest income. Being the lender is lucrative and can move you ahead quickly. There is nothing more fun than passive income and having the ability to support those you love in building visions, creating priceless experiences, walking through challenging times, and changing generational hardships!

> Only spend this money on things that will make you money!

The banks make a fortune funding these things in most people's lives, sometimes to the tune of hundreds of thousands of dollars on one loan. So make sure this money is coming back to you rather than to them. Maximize this recurring deposit percentage and work to increase it by even just 1 percent at every opportunity. When your money makes you money and doesn't require your time and energy, you no longer have a job; you have freedom! Remember that and work toward it every day like your life depends on it because not only does your life depend on it, but so does theirs.

This is the part of the book that gets me all giddy! I love to hear stories from people whose lives have been changed forever because a random person who took the time to build wealth decided to take a bet on them. I currently have a client whose landlord bet on her and her husband when they had to file for bankruptcy after their child became ill and the medical bills piled up. Accepting them as a tenant eventually turned into selling them the house, which they're now selling for a life-changing opportunity. Their house had appreciated so much that they were able to pay cash for their next home and live mortgage-free! This move will enable them to take care of their family without the need to work, following her husband's major heart attack at just fifty-two years old! In just six years, the equity built will allow them to never struggle again! This family can now be the bank for their loved ones and change the lives of future generations.

My mind was blown that the *yes* of someone who worked to have investments could forever change generations of a family they had barely met. Their landlord literally changed generations by investing in real estate and gaining the financial ability to be a blessing to others. How cool is that! I'm forever grateful to those who bet on me and changed my life in similar ways. How many other lives did they change? How many lives will be changed as *we* work to emulate the character they displayed? How many others will we bless? When you make the decision to be intentional about this journey, you will have no idea how far the blessings will reach.

L-iabilities/Lifestyle

Debts. Make a plan to pay off your debts. They should be a line item on your expense budget until you do. List them in order from highest interest rate to lowest and double up on payments on the high-rate lines of credit until they're paid off. Then, move that same payment amount to the lower-rate lines until they're paid off. Don't just move high-rate debt to lines of credit with lower rates.

So often, I hear people talk about moving high-rate debt balances to lower rates in order to lower payments, but the challenge is that it's a temporary solution to a long-term problem. While this might help at the moment (if you're committed to going all in and getting them paid), you also have to change the behavior that got you there in the first place. If you don't, you'll just end up with a bigger debt snowball and find yourself

> You also have to change the behavior that got you there in the first place.

searching for yet another low-rate, short-term fix. Eventually, all the open lines of credit, fees, and accounts will be overwhelming and too much to manage.

We can't continue robbing Peter to pay Paul so we can feel better for a moment. Remember that the wealthy generate income to buy assets that pay for their expenses and produce more income to buy more assets and generate more income. Think about that for a moment. Their assets generate income, so they don't have to; therefore, they get to work because they "want to," not because they "have to." The middle class uses their income to buy "things" first and assets with what is left, if anything is left. This strategy can work at times, but it never gets them out of the rat race com-

> Their assets generate income, so they don't have to; therefore, they get to work because they "want to," not because they "have to."

pletely. The broke use their income to pay for things beyond what they can afford and have nothing left. Even worse, they borrow on high-interest credit to buy more things, eventually digging a hole that is difficult to get out of (REFER TO THE HOW THE WEALTHY SPEND RESOURCE AT THE END OF THE CHAPTER).

So, what can we do? Change your thinking, change your life. Pay off bad debt and build capital to buy real cash-flowing assets that pay for themselves and eventually replace your need for job income. That's freedom! That's what you're working toward!

Taxes. If you're like I was, tax law is a "dirty word" in your house. I knew so little about the laws that I couldn't take advantage of them. That's not so true for me anymore. Over the years, I've learned that the tax laws are a guide to help me actually *keep* my money by using it in ways the government determines will stimulate the economy. The more I hated giving my money away, the more I worked to educate myself and find educated partners to help me on my wealth journey.

Take the time to learn about taxes and how to minimize them. Find an amazing accountant who understands real estate investing and connect with a great financial advisor. Don't stop looking until you find them. The best way to find them is to ask those around you who are winning at the wealth game for referrals. These people can be the golden key that saves you thousands of dollars and helps move you toward the financial future you desire. Make sure they know the tax code and ways to legitimately reduce your taxes in any way possible (not just get you standard deductions). Do you think Warren Buffett, Elon Musk, Jeff Bezos, and Donald Trump pay little to no taxes because they lie, cheat, and steal? Haha! Don't answer that; I was just getting your attention! I'd venture to bet it's because they have great tax advisors who have studied tax law and advise them on how to invest and flow their money so that they capitalize on the greatest tax benefits.

There are actually many wealthy people who pay little to no taxes. I encourage you to read the books on tax-free wealth. It's legal and a real thing! The tax code is designed to encourage money to flow through the economy. It's made to incentivize taxpayers to move their money through the things that the government needs to keep the economy strong. If you study and learn about where they want money to flow, you will find all kinds of incentives that will help you reduce one of the biggest expenses of your lifetime—taxes!

As I mentioned earlier, nearly 40–60 percent of your money will go to some type of tax in your lifetime. That's two million dollars per average American family. This number will only increase over time as the national debt grows. Imagine if you could take some of that money and give it to a cause you care about rather than giving it to Uncle Sam.

Make sure you budget for taxes and set that money aside and out of sight. This is definitely an area that can crumble and crush people. They fail to put money aside and then are hit with a huge tax bill. If the money is not there, the penalties and interest start accruing and snowballing, creating a massive issue. The government charges high rates when you have their money, and they want it, just like banks with credit card interest. Don't go there!

Y-early Income Needed

Once you have put the first five letters of the acronym together, the "Y" equals the "yearly income needed to live life by design."

F+A+M+I+L=Y BANK
YEARLY INCOME NEEDED TO LIVE LIFE BY DESIGN

Using the Action To Freedom worksheet, put your *freedom number* on line one (**REFER TO THE ACTION TO FREEDOM RESOURCE AT THE END OF THE CHAPTER**). Remember, your freedom number is the amount of passive income you need to fully satisfy your living expenses annually. This is your primary goal. Below it, list **three strategies** you will use to make it a reality, such as (1) earned income (wages, salaries, tips, commissions, etc.), (2) passive income (rental income, royalties, limited partnership income, etc.), and (3) investment income (interest income, profit share, dividends, etc.).

From there, list the **five priorities** that must hit your calendar regularly to execute this plan. Examples might include: (1) auto-deposit $500 per month in the S&P 500, (2) save $1,000 per month for a down payment on a rental, (3) send one hundred letters to absentee landlords looking for seller finance opportunities, (4) generate x-profit from sales monthly to add to investment account, and (5) spend two hours weekly (eight per month) looking for real estate opportunities. I would also suggest reading one book per month about money and real estate investing, having lunch with one mentor per week to learn how they created success, and meeting five new people per month who are thinking of selling or can teach you investment strategies. Make sure that you're willing to commit to whatever you list as a priority. If they're small, that's OK; just start. You can grow as you go.

Next, take your yearly-income-needed number (your freedom number) and divide it by twelve. That's your monthly income needed. Take that number and divide it by four weeks. That's what you have to bring in each week. Now, that number looks more reasonable, doesn't it? Focus on that!

> **Make sure the activities showing up on your calendar are priorities related to earning you that number.**

Every week, make sure the activities showing up on your calendar are priorities related to earning you *that* number. If they're not, remove the things that get in the way and add the ones that contribute. Say *no*, like we talked about earlier. If your income isn't to the point where you can invest yet, go back to the part of the book where we discussed how to maximize income and find opportunities. Remember, this book was written to guide you through a process. Go back, read again, adjust, and get focused! You'll get there!

Lastly, make sure you plug that number into the Break It Down worksheet I've provided so you can revisit it often and stay on track **(REFER TO THE BREAK IT DOWN RESOURCE AT THE END OF THE CHAPTER)**. If you live in a family with two incomes, do your best to live off just one. Save the other for investing and creating passive income. The goal is to get you to a point where you can work because you love to, not because you have to. Be sure the Red Light, Green Light "money date" activities happen monthly or at least quarterly. Put it on the calendar as a recurring appointment with your money. Audit your habits, money, and calendar at that time as well. Make adjustments. Check in regularly with your accountability partner. If you get off track, get back on before the snowball gets unmanageable and overwhelming. You won't be perfect at this. It's a living process used over time. It's a system that keeps you within the lines and can counterbalance your slipups before you're too far out of balance to make corrections.

Protect Your Assets

IMPORTANT information to help you get your personal stuff in order and protect your wishes and your assets:

(These things can vary a bit from state to state, so be sure to do your own research.)

LIST ACCOUNTS AND NUMBERS

Make a list of all banks, account numbers, investment accounts, credit cards, mortgage info, utilities, life insurance policies, etc. as well as due dates and how and when these things get paid.

BENEFICIARIES ON ALL ACCOUNTS

Make sure all bank accounts have beneficiaries listed. The beneficiary will only need your death certificate and an ID to access your funds.

IMPORTANT LOGIN INFO

Make a list of login info and be sure SOMEONE knows your Apple ID, bank ID/account logins, and passwords!

TITLES

Make sure you have titles for all vehicles, campers, boats, toys, etc.!

MEDICAL POWER OF ATTORNEY

This document allows you to designate someone to make healthcare decisions for you in the event you are unable to do so yourself.

DURABLE POWER OF ATTORNEY

This document allows you to designate someone to make legal decisions if you are unable or incompetent.

Protect Your Assets

LIVING WILL

A living will is a document that explains how you want things handled in the event you cannot communicate or make decisions due to illness or incapacity. It can include such things as healthcare preferences and other end-of-life decisions.

LAST WILL AND TESTAMENT

A last will and testament specifies how your personal belongings will be distributed and who your administrator will be. If you have a beneficiary on any of your financial accounts, that information will override a will. For example, if your will states you are leaving all possessions to your son, but an account indicates the beneficiary is your cousin, then that money goes to your cousin. Be sure your documents are congruent.

FUNERAL WISHES

Written funeral wishes will convey your preferences concerning burial, cremation, or other desires regarding the physical body and funeral services.

BENEFICIARY DEED

A beneficiary deed will transfer your home in the event of your passing. A title company can assist you in completing and filing this document, and it will save your heirs THOUSANDS. All they will need to sell your home is their ID and your death certificate. This will avoid the home having to go through probate.

SET UP A TRUST

Set up a trust for beneficiaries who are not of legal age and appoint a trustee.

Protect Your Assets

AT MINIMUM, list beneficiaries on all financial accounts, such as checking, savings, life insurance, investments, CDs, etc. Your heirs will then only need a death certificate and ID to get to your money. Make lists to give to a trusted person or spouse, or place them in a safe or in a security box at the bank. If your beneficiaries don't know you have a savings account at ABC Bank, they will not be able to access the money. Make sure you have a trusted person who is designated as a signer on the security box or who knows the passcode to the safe where you will keep the following information.

RESEARCH THE FOLLOWING:

LIFE ESTATES

Life estates allow you to sell a residence and retain use and occupancy of the property until your passing, when it will then transfer to the intended party.

REVERSE MORTGAGES

A reverse mortgage can be an option to help senior homeowners with living expenses. It will allow your heirs to sell the home and retain the equity at your passing or pay off the balance and keep the property. A reverse mortgage is not right for everyone, but it is worth researching and knowing your options.

If the above documents are completed, your heirs can AVOID probate. If not, accounts with money that don't have beneficiaries will go into an estate account set up by an attorney. The attorney will then publicize your passing in the newspaper, allowing anyone to make a claim on your property. Probate is costly and can be a complete PAIN in the butt. It's important to TALK with those close to you and make your wishes KNOWN. Let those you've designated know your intentions and why you chose them. Let those not designated understand your decisions as well. Explaining your decisions will help to avoid future questions and hurt feelings.

Family BANKING

The family banking system is an income generating system designed to create multiple streams of income, fund important family milestones, and buy cashflowing assets that exceed your FREEDOM number using real estate as the primary asset.

FAMILY BANK

Save & grow newfound money in your family bank. Put it in accounts that pay higher rates. Money from the family bank must be paid back with interest to grow or used to repeat steps four & five.

MAXIMIZE JOB INCOME

Be in the top 1% of a high-paying profession. Work for the promotion, overtime, bonus, side hustle, etc.

CASHFLOW TO BUY MORE ASSETS

Think of each asset as a business. It must pay its own expenses & generate profit. Use profit generated to pay down mortgages on assets or add to your family banking system to buy more income generating assets.

REPEAT STEPS 4, 5, & 10

REDUCE EXPENSES

Live below your means. Cut expenses, drop subscriptions, stop expensive habits, reduce rates on loans & LOC. Shop service prices and lower insurance costs.

BUY INCOME-PRODUCING ASSETS

Buy assets that will profit even in the worst-case scenario, not liabilities that steal from your accounts & feed your emotions. Live in them and do the work yourself when possible to leverage the best loans & keep equity.

RAISE PERSONAL CAPITAL

Add additional income streams to existing assets. Get licensed to generate referral income & keep commissions on purchases & sales. Leverage tax law to keep money. Sell things you don't really need or use. Be intentional not emotional!

*Family*BANKING *cont.*

REVERSE ENGINEER THE PLAN

Know your freedom number. Reverse engineer a plan that excites you & that you're willing to commit to. Track your net worth & your cashflow, including the value of your businesses.

INVEST IN RELATIONSHIPS

Work on your people skills, learn to listen and ask great questions, and genuinely care about others. This opens the door to valuable partnership opportunities.

BECOME A STUDENT OF WEALTH

Be a student of wealth, tax law, and the economy so that you understand how they work together.

BE GENEROUS

Always leave people better than you found them. Tithe by giving your time, money, and knowledge, thereby adding value to others.

HOW THE *Wealthy* SPEND

The difference between the wealthy and the broke is how they spend!

The **WEALTHY** generate income to buy income generating assets that pay for their expenses, buy them things, and generate more income to buy more assets.

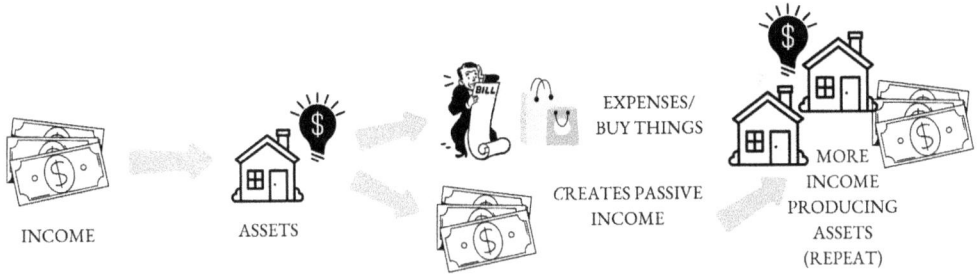

INCOME — ASSETS — EXPENSES/BUY THINGS — CREATES PASSIVE INCOME — MORE INCOME PRODUCING ASSETS (REPEAT)

The **MIDDLE CLASS** use their income to pay expenses and buy things first. They may eventually buy an asset with what is left.

INCOME — EXPENSES/BUY THINGS — *EVENTUAL* ASSETS

The **BROKE** use their money to pay expenses.

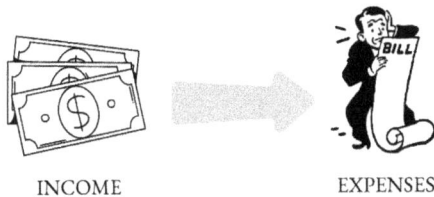

INCOME — EXPENSES

ACTION TO FREEDOM

Taking your freedom number and breaking it down to an executable plan.

1 Goal - Annual Freedom Number

\#

3 Strategies for achieving it

1   *2*   *3*

Five priorities that *need* to happen regularly

1

2

3

4

5

BREAK IT DOWN

Writing down your goals and breaking them into bite-size pieces makes them actionable. Start week one with tasks that will help you meet your monthly goal and ultimately lead to your annual goal. During weeks two, three, and four, adjust as needed based on activities completed the previous week.

ANNUAL GOAL

MONTHLY GOAL

WEEK 1	WEEK 2	WEEK 3	WEEK 4

Chapter 16

BANKING SYSTEM

Systematize the process so it happens easily.

WHEN YOU'RE PREPARED FOR THE BUMPS,
THEY DON'T SEEM SO BIG.

"Many people have the capacity to make enough money to live
comfortably, but they are afraid to step out of their comfort zones.
Often, this is because, when they first do that, they are not prepared to
go forward. I don't want them to be too scared to try, but they should
be prepared to encounter bumps in the road and then go forward."

—Grandma Clare

AS YOU GAIN CLARITY ON YOUR PLAN and start building systems to support it, think about setting up your physical accounting system so that it
pays you first and alerts you when things are off track. I recommend that you
systemize your savings.

One of the best things I've done for myself is to create a system with my
bank accounts that allows me to see at a glance how well I am managing.
This system also allows for exponential growth by simply keeping the
money out of sight and out of mind. It forces me to operate within the
budget I created. To ensure this system supports my plan, I set up multiple
bank accounts and pay myself first.

Let me explain. Through the money activities discussed in the previous chapters, I've learned that my **monthly essential and optional expenses** (Green and Yellow expenses) are 40 percent of my average monthly income. (Please be aware that your personal percentage will differ from mine and will be based on completing the money activities discussed earlier.) Beginning with that number, I complete the following steps:

1. When a paycheck comes in, I deposit the entire check into my **income account**. That's where *all* income goes.

2. Immediately, I calculate and transfer 40 percent of the check (my expense budget number) out to another account called my **expense account**. This is where *all* spending happens. This transaction takes about two seconds to complete. (Remember, profit stays behind in the income account, so I'm essentially paying myself first!)

3. I then calculate 30 percent of what's left in the income account as the amount I'll owe for taxes (If you do the math, this equates to 18% of the *total* paycheck). I immediately transfer that amount from my income account to my **taxes account**. I do this because I own rentals and am self-employed. Taxes are not automatically taken from the "paychecks" I receive. Forgetting this piece could destroy me (and you) at tax time.

4. The remaining money in the income account is essentially profit and gets distributed to one or more of the following three **"abundance accounts"** I'm intentionally working to fund:

   a. **Emergency Account:** I keep a minimum of $3,000 in this account. This pays for unexpected expenses, like the car breaking down or having to fix a refrigerator fail. This account will cover most sudden and unexpected expenses. Once my emergency account has a balance of $3,000 to $5,000, the balance in my income account then starts funding my reserve account and my Family Bank account.

   b. **Reserve Account** - When my emergency account is fully funded, I begin funding my reserve account. This account equals four to six months of essential and optional expenses. It will pay all monthly expenses in case I am unable to make income for some time. No one thinks jobs can end or emergencies can happen until they do.

c. **Family Bank Account** - The Family Bank account and the reserve account may be funded simultaneously, with the money being split between the two. Unlike the emergency and reserve accounts, the Family Bank continues to be funded forever. The purpose of this account is to fund an abundant life!

As your emergency and reserve accounts become fully funded, your Family Bank will continue to be funded with the balance of the income account. Your emergency and reserve accounts protect your Family Bank account (your future) from being blindly spent, as can happen when your money is located in a single checking or bank account. This fund grows quickly and serves as a savings for goals and investments. It will grow faster than you think and is fun to watch! Soon, the down payment for your first rental property or money to start up that business will be sitting there, ready to multiply and make you more.

There are two important rules to follow concerning your Family Bank account:

1. Make it your mission to only use this money to buy things that *pay* you and appreciate. Spend 80 percent on income-generating items and 20 percent or less on other things you need or want, paying that money back with interest to the account. Don't let it all go toward depreciating items.

2. If you borrow from it, auto-deposit a set payment amount from each check back into it until it's paid back with interest. This automatic payment should come from your expense account and be a line item on your budget because it's a loan. If you don't make it automatic, you're less likely to actually do it. You can then grow this account and make it a source of cash flow by buying investments that will fund "fun" and quality of life forever while also giving you back the time that is currently spent at your J.O.B. You can also earmark money within your Family Bank account by adding more specific

accounts, such as "debt reduction" or "vacation fund." You may choose to be even more specific and nickname them according to the current goal—for example, "beach condo down payment."

Yes, you can have fun, lots of it; just plan it! As I've said before, I encourage you to schedule that trip as a reward for your hard work, even put it on the calendar, and prepay a portion the year before. Then you're committed and can't make excuses not to go. It's also partially paid for, so it doesn't break the bank. You need fun and rest in your life! It can't be all about the hustle.

Below are the six accounts I've used over the years and a visual of how your money flows through them (REFER TO THE MONEY FLOW RESOURCE AT THE END OF THIS CHAPTER).

1. Income: where all income is deposited
2. Expense: 40 percent of income (where all expenses are paid)
3. Taxes: 30% of net profit (30 percent of what's left after expenses are paid)

The remaining balance goes into your three "abundance" buckets below. Remember to prioritize the emergency fund and then fund the others.

4. Emergency: (fund first) $3,000 to $5,000 in case of emergency
5. Reserve: (fund next) four to six months of essential and optional expenses in case of a recession, job loss, or other negative financial events
6. Family Bank/Goals: (fund forever) funds for investments, down payments for homes, specific goals, and yearly trips using the 80/20 rule

Once the emergency and reserve accounts are funded, the Family Bank will receive the bulk of the income account balance and grow rapidly. Based on your preference, the Family Bank can be set up as a separate account as described above, or its funds can simply be left in the income account to grow. I choose to leave the Family Bank money in my income account so that my bank doesn't charge me monthly for a zero balance after all funds are dispersed.

The thing I love about this system is it requires that you have a vision and a plan and that you prioritize. And even if you're not looking at a detailed report, you quickly know when you're over budget for the month. When you get a low-balance alert in your expense account and have to pull money from your Family Bank account to cover it, it will cause a visceral reaction in your gut. You will immediately know that you have overspent and are borrowing from your family's future money. This will make you feel a little annoyed with yourself and ready to be frugal for the rest of the month. The great thing about this system is that you know there is a problem immediately versus a month or two later when you finally get your profit and loss report (if you even have one) using traditional bookkeeping.

> When you get a low-balance alert in your expense account and have to pull money from your Family Bank account to cover it, it will cause a visceral reaction in your gut.

If your expense budget is well over 40 percent of your income, work each month to bring it down just 1 percent until you're where you want to be. When your Family Bank account is keeping all 30 percent or more of your checks each month, and your tax account and reserve account are fully funded, there will be no stress when writing the check for taxes at the end of the year. Instead, you'll find that you have money to move the ball forward on the next step of that life you're designing. You will also find that 30 percent put aside for taxes is likely overkill, and you will have money left over to move back to the Family Bank account at the end of the year.

MONEY *flow* ACCOUNT DIAGRAM

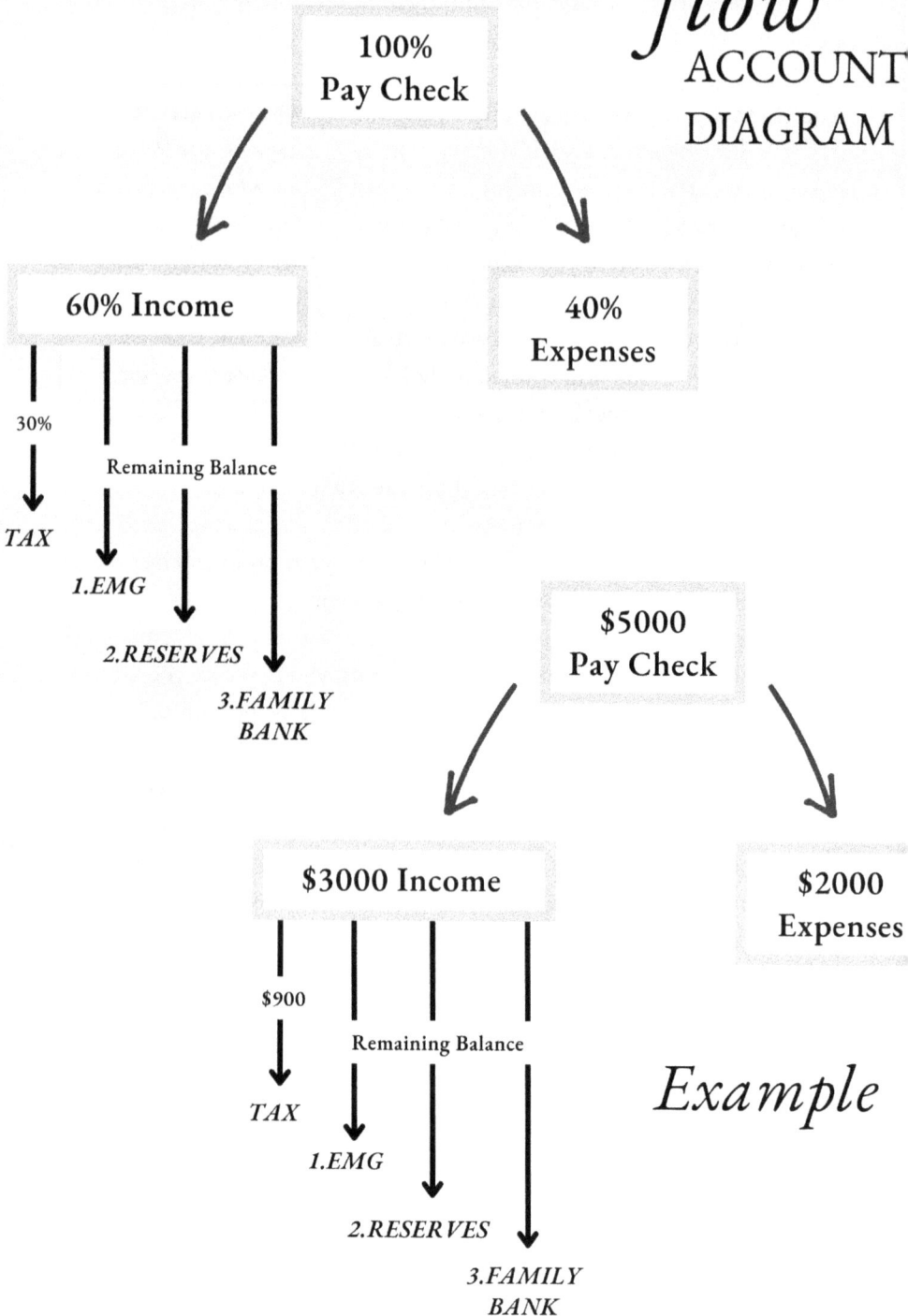

100% Pay Check

60% Income

40% Expenses

30%

Remaining Balance

TAX

1.EMG

2.RESERVES

3.FAMILY BANK

$5000 Pay Check

$3000 Income

$2000 Expenses

$900

Remaining Balance

TAX

1.EMG

2.RESERVES

3.FAMILY BANK

Example

Chapter 17

YES

Define what gets a *yes*.

TO WIN AT ANYTHING, YOU HAVE TO have clarity about what you want and a definitive formula for a "yes." Over the years, I've created a formula for analyzing properties that work for my goals. Although my formula may be too conservative for some investors, it supports the risk tolerance my husband and I feel comfortable with. It's a formula that makes it easier to move quickly, keeps us safe from extremely high-risk investments, and defines a "no" without wasting much time. I'm not here to tell you this is the *only* formula. It's simply the one I've used successfully over the years. As wealth is created, risk tolerance can be carefully adjusted. The point is to have a baseline from which to make decisions. This will help you move logically and eliminate emotional decisions that increase the probability of disaster. We had rules when we started, and many of them still hold true now, even though we have a portfolio with a significant amount and cash flow that provides independence **(REFER TO THE DO'S AND DON'TS RESOURCE AT THE END OF THIS CHAPTER).**

One great project can change everything!

"One trajectory that benefited me was the Arizona State Land Department auction when I put a down payment on 120 acres. Jack and I were stalled. We wanted to subdivide, but the city of Flagstaff was requiring that we put millions into offsite sewer and water systems.

We didn't have the money. So, we held the property for a few years. And guess what? The head of the Flagstaff zoning department presented us with an offer from the adjacent Continental Country Club. As it tripled our original cost, we accepted it. We decided to exchange part of the piece for buildable property in the city. The members of the country club group were agreeable. I found nine acres in a rundown area, only 500 feet from Northern Arizona University. The country club owners acquired it and had it zoned commercial before we exchanged it. I should have kept ten acres of the country club land and would advise anyone selling to a big developer to keep a portion. On our nine acres of commercial property, we began a family legacy.

The tenants were Social Security, McCracken Realty (me), and a local state agency. We borrowed $100,000 to complete it.

Two years later, the Arizona Department of Economic Security contracted with us. They needed to consolidate their Flagstaff services. We expanded to 17,000 feet, and they moved in. Later, they took over the Social Security space, and we leased to them for forty-three years to the tune of $25,000 per month, which changed our lives and the lives of future generations."

—Grandma Clare

Here are some of the rules we've lived by:

1. Hustle to earn, liquidate, and mine for excess cash in order to acquire instant equity, passive income, and tax shelters that multiply your funds. That old saying, "Do it as though your life depends on it," should be taken seriously during the season when you're working to gain capital.

2. Don't risk the farm! Never risk the roof that protects your family. We were always willing to use equity from other assets (although we never actually had to), but the roof over our family was off-limits.

3. Only invest with partners you know, love, and trust, and keep them short-term until you have completed a few deals and know that you operate well together. Who and what you invest in are often more

important than the investment itself. There will always be more opportunities.

4. Hunt for opportunity and time block it! Have more conversations where you are listening and looking for pain or pleasure. Look for clues, send the letters, drive the neighborhoods, post the ads, get on the wholesale lists, talk to agents, and stop at the garage sales. Have eyes and ears out hunting deals for you. It's worth paying others. They could end up finding a deal that will change your life!

5. Always have more than one exit strategy. You won't win them all, and when you lose, you want to exit with the least amount of pain possible.

> **Always have more than one exit strategy.**

6. Defend the deal. For every deal you think you find, analyze it and find three more to compare it to. You'll begin to quickly identify your favorite deal types and see them everywhere. Live by the rule: If the numbers don't make sense, don't do the deal. One of our greatest challenges in this game is that our emotions start making decisions and overriding the math and logic.

7. Play the long game. If you are comfortable with your answers, go for it. You're not betting money that will destroy your life, and you have to take calculated risks to get to the rewards. You have done the work; you can bet on yourself! You're not getting any younger, and building wealth is a long game, so get going!

Although you will have to make calculated risks while investing, when deals pop up, limit your risk by considering the following:

1. Ballpark the *1 percent rule* AVR(after repair value) to see if it's even worth going down that bunny hole. Will it return 1 percent of the after-repair price monthly or very close to it? This might be difficult to do if prices are high in your area, so be prepared to look outside your immediate market.

2. Do you have 25 percent down? Most traditional financing will require it, and truthfully, you want at least that much equity to safe-

guard you from market shifts that could make you upside down on your purchase.

3. Will the investment fund itself? You never want to rob one investment or business to pay for another. Each should have its own profit and loss and be self-funding.

4. Will it make its own payment if rents were to drop by 50 percent? It sounds excessive, but you'll thank me when it happens. So many new investors bet on short-term ideas without considering historical changes in the market or the temporary market they're betting on.

5. Can you add value to make it worth significantly more or produce more cash flow? Can you add square footage or improve the functionality of the floor plan? Be aware of neighborhood comps, and don't overimprove the property. Many investors lose their profit by turning a property into what they like versus what's applicable for the neighborhood.

6. Is there a higher, better use? Look at use and zoning. Can it bring in more if you change its use—a single-family to a multifamily or a large acreage to multiple lots with homes, or maybe even residential to commercial? What's the growth in the area? Is there a better use?

7. Will the owner/seller carry the note? Can you creatively finance the repairs into the loan to keep your personal cash liquid? If the numbers make sense, can you entice the seller by showing them the benefits of earning interest and avoid the headache of traditional financing?

8. If they carry the note, can the profit from rental income be put aside in an income-generating account to pay the balloon in full? Don't end up on the other side of "no plan!" It can cost you everything.

9. Would you want to own it in ten years if you had to? Can you use it personally and leverage tax law in some way?

10. Is the property in the path of progress?

11. Is it close enough for you to keep your eyes on, or do you have someone you trust who can? Start with assets you can keep your eyes on and learn what is required before you leverage others. This will help you know what to hold them accountable to.

12. Are there any imminent, big-ticket expenses you're not considering—roof replacements, old plumbing, electrical, or HVAC? Would a home warranty help with these?

13. If you're short of money and have the time, can you do some of the work yourself?

14. Do you know where the property lines are?

15. Have you looked at the property use rules and restrictions?

16. Do the *real* numbers make sense when you put everything into the Investment Calculator **(REFER TO THE RENTAL INVESTMENT CALCULATOR RESOURCE AT THE END OF THIS CHAPTER)?** One of the biggest mistakes investors make is not calculating all-in costs. They trick themselves into believing the return is higher than it is because they're emotionally excited. Remember, you can always adjust your offer. All they can say is no. It's just a numbers game. Ask enough times, and you'll get a yes!

> **Do the real numbers make sense?**

17. Do you have other investment options to compare it to so you can defend the deal to investor partners, lenders, and your spouse? This is a safety-net practice you should adopt, even if you're just defending the deal to yourself.

18. Ask yourself what the worst possible outcome is. Can you live with it if it were to happen?

19. Do your research, ask lots of questions, and listen for inconsistencies.

"It's a no-brainer to buy land in the path of progress. My family has done that often. When that land was sold, I always kept a piece, preferably a corner, that the developer would have to utilize to bring in utilities and roads. I have often regretted not thinking of that when we sold the large parcel to the local country club owners! Next, inspect, inspect, inspect, and do all of your due diligence! Years ago, we were looking at a ranch for sale. Much of the value was in the water rights and land to feed the cattle. The seller showed us a field that was a mile from the irrigation well and actually ran the water for a short time.

After closing the escrow, we couldn't figure out how to irrigate that field. We were victims of fraud by the seller. The field was not irrigatable. We had to go back and take him to court and win the lawsuit. We were able to deduct the monies from the mortgage. It was a huge hassle and a lesson learned. I really believe we won when the lawyer asked each of us, 'How many court cases have you had?' It was our first, and we said so. The seller replied, 'Several, it's a way of doing business.' Always require a survey on land. Quite often, corners can be moved. In fact, we caught a forest service employee in the act of moving a section corner years ago. Zoning: do not take the word of the person at the counter. Get a copy of the rezoning codes and then read them and read them again. The same goes for HOAs and deed restrictions. I was once threatened with an HOA fine because I put a bluebird house in my front yard. I liked it, and it helped my friends find my house.

Deed restrictions are often invalid after twenty years, but not always. Often, they are ignored until some kind of conflict occurs. Again, read them and inquire. Doing the research ahead of time has been invaluable. Neglecting it often causes allegations to raise their ugly heads."

—Grandma Clare

DOS & DON'TS

There are a lot of investment gurus out there. Be sure you're learning from one with a similar risk tolerance and verified proof of success.

DO THIS	DON'T DO THIS
Hustle to earn, liquidate, and mine for excess cash	Assume you're broke and there's no waste in your spending
Only bet what you can afford to lose	Risk the farm
Only invest with partners you know, love, and trust	Partner for the opportunity without vetting the partners
Hunt for opportunity	Assume there's limited opportunity and it's not for you
Limit your risk using the questions on p. 33	Act out of emotion and buy something because you think you might lose it
Always have more than one exit strategy	Buy something you can't rent or sell to someone if you need out
If the numbers don't make sense, don't do the deal	Use haphazard math without running the real numbers
Play the long game	Try to get rich quick

RENTAL INVESTMENT
Calculator

Scan to use
one for yourself!

Purchase

Purchase Price	$200,000
Use Loan? ● Yes No	
Down Payment	20%
Interest Rate	6%
Loan Term	30 years
Closing Cost	$6,000
Need Repairs?	Yes ● No

Recurring Operating Expenses

		Annual Increase
Monthly Rent	$2,000	3%
Total Insurance	$0	3%
HOA Fee	5	3%
Maintenance Fee	0%	3%

Recurring Operating Expenses

	Annual	Annual Increase
Property Tax	$3,000	3%
Total Insurance	$1,200	3%
HOA Fee	$0	3%
Maintenance	$2,000	3%
Other Costs	$500	3%

Sell

Do You Know the Sell Price?
   Yes ● No

Value Appreciation	3%	per year
Holding Length	20	years
Cost to Sell	8%	

Calculate ▶

Example

Chapter 18

BUSY

Don't be too *busy* to be successful.

YOU'RE GOING TO NEED TIME TO RUN the investment plays, and not every opportunity will be a yes! Remember, when you say *yes* to something, you're sacrificing and saying *no* to something else—another opportunity, another relationship, or another investment. With the same number of hours in the day as those who succeed and win massively in this life, you must make sure you don't waste minutes being "busy" and pretending you're accomplishing things, like so many others. To live your life by design, you must make sure your calendar and bank statements show your commitment to your plan. If you tell me you want to build passive income through investing, there should be time blocks in your calendar reserved for learning and doing just that. Even fifteen minutes a day will change your life. The seasons in life when I was too busy to hunt for opportunities or see them when they were right in front of me were the seasons that yielded the least returns. Don't be too busy to be successful! You must make time to hunt, educate, connect, analyze, and just get better. It's a numbers game; if it were easy, everyone would be wealthy.

> Don't be too busy to be successful!

The issue we face is "good intentions." We get a "Got a minute?" call from someone who needs us, and we love to feel needed. It boosts our self-confidence, so we say yes. We get a call from someone else with an idea or a project. From their perspective, we're the perfect fit. So we say yes, flattered that they thought of us. Instantly, we are off and running in a direction that takes us off our own path and plan. So often, our yeses are not aligned with our mission, and even worse, they distract us from reaching our goals. And as we've discussed earlier, in some cases, they're with the wrong people.

After many failures, I learned that you never say yes to an opportunity just because the opportunity sounds good. You must *only* say yes to opportunities that are (1) in alignment with your goals and (2) involve the right people. If there is one but not the other, the answer is a big *no*! Don't waste lots of time and money going in circles with the wrong opportunities and the wrong people because you're searching for something that makes you happy without knowing exactly what that is.

Who you're in business with matters!

"The worst traumatic messes that I've encountered were second mortgages, where I was stupid enough to give a big developer a chance to mortgage property that I was selling. A second mortgage enabled them to get a first mortgage on the property and allowed us to proceed to build projects. However, we learned that their goal was not just to finance a building but was often to avoid paying the second mortgage. I learned that I could not trust big developers who tried to evade payment by threatening to stop paying the first mortgage so that I would be stuck paying back the millions that they had borrowed against my former property, an amount I would not have the resources to repay. I was frustrated and really afraid that I would lose large amounts of time and money. We tried, but I had to choose between giving up substantial income, which my husband and I had worked for years to amass, or calling their bluff and agreeing to pay off the mortgages, which I really had no way of accomplishing. But I did it. I told my people to tell the developer that I would take over the million-dollar mortgages and property. The developers backed down, and we got paid our money. I learned not to ever get in that position again. Many people I know have been cheated out of money because they were generous enough to OK a second mortgage."

—Grandma Clare

A few years back, I said yes to a business opportunity where I was super passionate about the role and the company. Flattered that I was chosen as the token person to move the company forward, I was blinded by the opportunity, even though I knew that the core values of the other partners didn't match mine. I invested my time and lots of money to join the adventure. I was so excited to be a part of rebuilding a company I was passionate about that I failed to acknowledge the risk of being in business with the wrong people. After less than a year, the cookie finally crumbled to the tune of lawsuits, lies, and deception. I was behind on my life-by-design plan because I'd gone all in on theirs. I then spent another year of time and money hiring attorneys, wiping tears, and preparing for lawsuits. This is not something I ever want to waste my life or money on again.

The worst part about these situations is that you not only lose the time and money you invested in building their business but also years of time and money you could have used to move your life and ideas forward. You get robbed of the energy to enjoy life, family, and experiences because you're mentally broken and exhausted.

The moral of the story is to always trust your gut. Only say yes to relationships that give you love and results. Only agree to opportunities that align with your

> **Always trust your gut.**

goals and your values. You must be able to love your partner and together get results that lead you toward *your* goals. If that's not the case, they should not show up on your calendar or as a part of your profit and loss! Just remember, your time, energy, and money have a limit. They are finite. The life you have at the moment is a result of the way you manage your time, money, and relationships. If you're not getting what you want, adjust what you're doing. You're the designer of your life.

Though my story is about business opportunities and partners, the truth is that it's about anything and anyone that directly or indirectly consumes your time, money, or energy. What is currently taking place in your day that is eating up your precious minutes and keeping you from moving your dreams forward? Time is the only thing you can never get back. You're closer to the end of life than you have ever been, and you may not have used your time to move you closer to living your purpose. Think about that for a minute. Time is like money. You may feel like you're not making any big investments that will harm you. The small spends don't put a noticeable dent in your bank account. But, like a few minutes here and there on social media, it's those "small spends," those seemingly insignificant minutes that rob you the most because you never feel them until they're gone. Your time is even more valuable than your money, so be careful who and what you allow to consume it.

As we begin to close out our learning together, let's recap the path, starting from where you are now to the impact you will intentionally create in yourself and others.

Chapter 19

CHANGE

Change your thinking; change your life.

A LIFE BY DESIGN REQUIRES YOU TO THINK DIFFERENTLY.

BY NOW, I'M SURE YOU'RE STARTING TO realize that to become someone with different habits, you must first think differently. What got you here won't get you there. It's silly to believe that if you keep thinking, speaking, and acting in the same ways you always have, you will get something new. Wrong. You will get what you have always gotten. Reading a book and being inspired is great, but it's all wasted time if it's not followed by action that changes you and, even more importantly, your kids, those you love, and future generations. That's a pretty exciting and honorable responsibility you just can't take lightly. Start by simply recognizing the thoughts, relationships, and environments that don't serve you, and then decide to start making changes. Replace them with thoughts, words, and environments that do. Sometimes, it helps to visualize the person you want to become **(REFER TO THE BECOMING RESOURCE AT THE END OF THE CHAPTER).** Ask yourself who that person would surround themselves with. Where would they hang out? How would someone like them (someone winning at that level) speak to themselves and others?

> Start by simply recognizing the thoughts, relationships, and environments that don't serve you, and then decide to start making changes.

So, what do you need to do differently to change your life?

Become a business owner: If you're not a business owner, I highly recommend you consider a side hustle. This should not be something that distracts you from your primary earnings but something that adds revenue, creates tax savings opportunities, and has a higher dollar-per-hour rate that could eventually become a better career path.

Something as simple as a real estate license (for the purpose of sending referrals to other agents and keeping your commission when buying investments) can easily add the equivalent of your primary income to your annual earnings, and you never even have to sell a house! Not only do you get a good chunk of cash by connecting friends and family to a great agent, but you also get some great tax deductions or, even better, a down payment on your next investment!

I just popped by a friend's house last week, and she commented that her six-figure job cost her $50,000 in taxes this year, and on top of that, she will be paying over $60,000 in real estate fees between selling and buying her next home. I'm sure if she had thought about it beforehand, ninety hours of licensing classes and an exam would have been a small sacrifice to make to keep $110,000 in her bank account. Granted, she couldn't write off everything, but she could have drastically reduced her taxable income and collected a commission on the sale and purchase of her homes. She could have also made future passive income by connecting friends with great agents.

Create simple, powerful habits: A life by design is about creating simple, powerful habits, improving on them daily in small, sustainable ways, and creating rhythms that support and protect your mission. It's about prioritizing what matters most and getting better each day at moving the ball forward. It requires you to stop checking "things" off the list and start checking "priorities" off the list.

Being a people pleaser and saying yes to everything robs you of time, energy, and life. Make everything you do simple. Simple is executable! Execution done consistently rewards you with compound growth in all areas of your life, such as health, wealth, relationships, and spirituality. Be self-aware of the excuses you often make and the lies you tell yourself to justify your current actions. You're in control of your thoughts. Your job is to remind your brain who's boss and retrain it to believe you are that new person and that it's been wrong about you. Your consistent, small actions will prove this and reinforce your new habits.

Don't let this be something you dread. Make it fun. Gamify and create simple routines around the habits you'd like to create. Block your anticipated excuses before they come up. Track and measure your progress.

> Gamify and create simple routines around the habits you'd like to create.

Think of little hacks and games you can play with yourself to get things done. For instance, you don't get your first cup of Joe until your workout is complete. You don't get up from the computer for a break until you have accomplished a set task that moves the ball forward. If you're still avoiding doing what needs to be done, break it down into something smaller that you will do and build on over time. Reward yourself with that weekend staycation once you have met a significant benchmark. Eat a treat meal out only after you have packed your lunch for the whole week.

If we have the habit of rewarding ourselves when we haven't done the job, we train our minds, like spoiled children, to think we can have what we want when we want, with no responsibility in the process. (And we all know what happens to spoiled children.) You're literally hurting yourself every time you reward yourself without keeping your commitment. You're teaching your brain that you're not a person who keeps promises, and it will start believing you will never change. Prove it wrong. Don't reinforce those beliefs.

Create regular rhythms: Something as simple as a morning routine to start you off right, both physically and mentally, will make a huge difference in your life *and* finances! Think time to reflect on what's going well and where you need to adjust, which is priceless. Quiet time is necessary to move life forward in this noisy world.

Feed your body the fuel it needs to be physically healthy so it can keep up with you and your goals throughout the day. Have easy, healthy options on hand, just in case your day shifts. Then, you won't give in to fast and easy options that are unhealthy and hinder the performance of your mind and body. Stop eating foods that make you feel terrible, and cut down on drinking and other bad habits that abuse your body. Water, clean foods, sleep, and movement should be a part of your daily routine.

Have a money rhythm. Meet with your money monthly; make sure you're winning! Know what your goals are and how you are performing. Be sure you're paying payments on time. And remember, when leveraging other people's money (OPM), be it the banks, private lenders, or money from partners (which can be one of the fastest ways to grow your portfolio and build generational wealth), no one is going to trust you with their money if you can't be trusted with your own.

> No one is going to trust you with their money if you can't be trusted with your own.

Gamify living below your means.

"I have always had questions about generational wealth. How can I ensure that my children and grandchildren will be able to enjoy comfortable financial lives? They have to be motivated. I am still frugal. I buy from thrift stores, rarely spend $5 for a cup of gourmet coffee, and plan my meals around grocery bargains, yet I guess I'm a millionaire. To me, finding bargain treasures and trips is a fun hobby. My oldest daughter remembers the early years when we had mostly venison jerky gravy for dinner because we were saving so that we could have $10,000 for a bond and Jack could get his contractor license. To this day, she still enjoys the hobby of finding treasures and thrift stores, even though she and her husband are in the upper 2 percent of the national financial ratings. I believe that motivation to save money is easier when you have experienced going without. It is more difficult to train children of affluence to be moderate, so make it fun."

—Grandma Clare

Habits are all about your ability to control your thoughts, which control your emotions, which control your actions. Motivational speaker Jim Rohn said, "There are two types of pain you will go through in this life: the pain of discipline and the pain of regret. Discipline weighs ounces, while regret weighs tons." Don't give in to the "I want it now" and "I deserve it" thoughts; that's what undisciplined people do. That just enables you to continue bad behaviors and get unwanted results. Being undisciplined trains your brain to believe that you don't have to do the activities to get the results. That's a lie! That's how people become addicted, overweight, broke, divorced, and stressed, like the Joneses.

Anything worth having requires effort. By starting with yourself and controlling and improving your actions, you can control your life's trajectory. You'll look back after only a short period of time and be mind-blown at what you have accomplished and what you're capable of. It's not about perfection; it's about consistent, small, compounding actions. In 2 Timothy 1:7, the Bible reminds us that God did not give us a spirit of fear but of power, love, and *self-control.*

Effort, like money, grows over time. It's not a linear growth; it's a compounding result **(REFER TO THE COMPOUND RETURNS RESOURCE AT THE END OF THIS CHAPTER).** Your actions create a result, and over time, the habit becomes a part of who you are. If you're struggling to make a change, break it down into small steps and just start with something, even if it's only ten minutes a day. Once you have the hang of something and it takes little to no thought or effort, you can scale it. Work toward 1 percent improvements in the areas of your life where you need to see change and create exponential growth. The key is not the size of the activity but the consistency around it.

Seek improvement in the following areas and create habits that lead to exponential growth:

- Your thoughts and words: An occasional positive thought or word can have a linear impact, but it won't make a massive change. Consistent positive thoughts and words change you and how you see yourself. The result is compounded in how you show up and who you become.
- Your relationships: An occasional friendly greeting or act of kindness in passing on a busy day is nice, but it will not impact those around you and will not make long-lasting change. Intentionally nurture and make time for positive relationships. Consistently investing in the lives of others will reward you and them greatly. Choose relationships that give you energy, match

your core values, and make you a better person. Be open to relationships where people think differently and challenge you, for they create growth. God intended for us to continually grow into our purpose and use that talent to bless others. And remember, the right relationships generate the greatest opportunities. The wealth in life is in relationships, and the multiplying of great relationships is where abundance and happiness are found.

- Your health: An occasional healthy meal is good, but it won't improve your health in the long run. A habit of eating well over time can result in positive changes to your weight, your energy, and your brain health. It's a compound result. Take care of this one body you have been given so that you can enjoy your life by design for many years to come.

- Your money: Occasionally, adding $100 to your mattress money is a great start but is slow linear growth. Adding an auto-deposit of the same amount to an account that pays you creates a vastly different compound return with the same deposits. Meet with your money regularly and make sure it is working for you.

- Your business: Doing something yourself gives you a linear return. Getting good at something and then teaching and hiring others to do it with you produces a compounding result with exponential benefit.

- Your investments: Buying a single-family home that pays you passive income is wonderful, but reinvesting that income to buy multiple homes, a multifamily complex, or even a mobile home park pays you exponentially. If you want to build passive income through investing, make sure you have time blocks in your calendar reserved for learning and doing just that. A few minutes a day of purposeful wealth-building actions will change your life.

We want compound returns, not linear returns. We want enough to make an impact, not just enough to be a little better off. We want to scale so our efforts can bless others, not just ourselves.

Run the model, and you'll take the guesswork out of building generational wealth, as seen in the Family Banking resource. You'll find that the Family Banking System becomes a perpetual cycle. It's not something you just start and finish. It's a system that becomes a habit—multiplying money and funding your preferred life.

> We want to scale so our efforts can bless others, not just ourselves.

- Maximize job income.
- Reduce expenses.
- Raise personal capital.
- Buy income-producing assets.
- Create cash flow to buy more assets.
- Use tax-advantaged Family Bank.
- Know the plan, track, and adjust.
- Invest in relationships.
- Be a student of wealth.
- Be generous.

BECOMING

Visualize and write out in vivid detail the life, business, income, and relationships you would like to have and the person you would be proud to be five years from now. How does that person spend their time, who do they spend it with, what do they contribute to others, where are they living and traveling, why do they believe in themselves, and who else is winning because they are winning?

Compound RETURNS

Things that compound have significant growth over time. Be sure you're spending your time and money in places that create compound versus linear returns.

■ Mattress ■ Real Estate ■ S & P 500

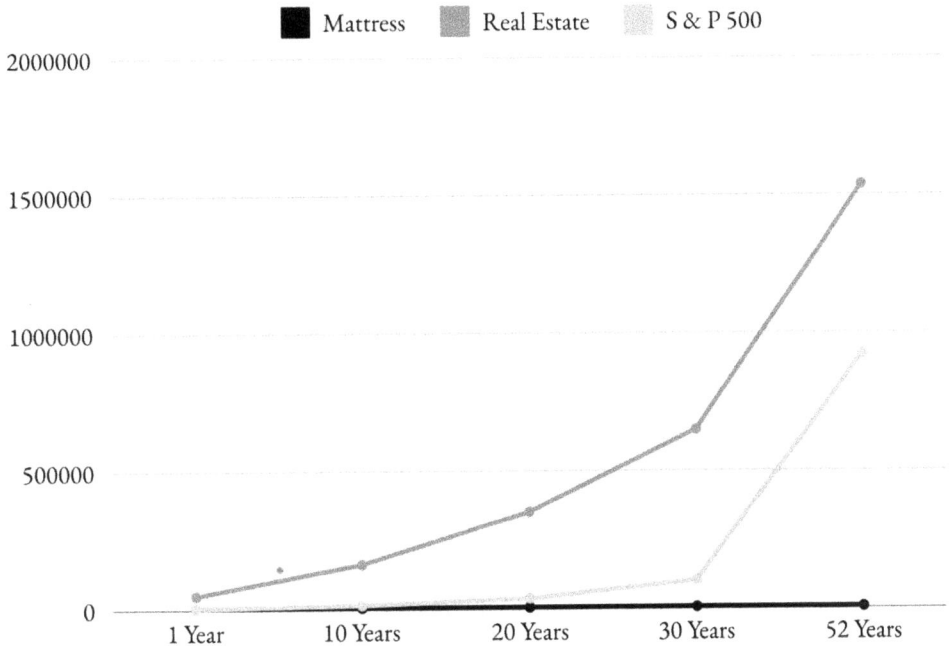

$5000 HELD DIFFERENTLY

MATTRESS i.e., INCOME EARNED
This is the actual money earned but has no growth because it is saved and not invested

REAL ESTATE/RENTAL i.e., INCOME PRODUCING ASSETTS
When money invested is earning income to pay for the asset and appreciation growth.

S&P 500 i.e., COMPOUND INTEREST EARNING
When interest is earned on both invested amount & on the interest earned over time.

.

Chapter 20

IMPACT

Make *impact* a multiplication, not just addition.

SOON, YOU WILL LOOK BACK AND REALIZE that the life you're living is the life you built by design. You'll finally have the time and money to bless those you love. Others will comment, "Must be nice to live your life." But don't let anyone make you feel bad for taking control of your circumstances and bettering yourself. Don't let them shame you for enjoying the time and talents God gave you, and remember not to collect the rewards just for yourself. Make sure to share them with others and make a real impact!

Make sure you're taking the time to teach your kids and loved ones these things. Be purposeful about blocking time to listen to podcasts and read books to help them grow into these understandings. Keep growing and stay ahead of those you love so that you can always lead and teach them. After all, if you are growing and not taking those around you along for the ride, you are robbing them of an opportunity to become their best selves. If you fail to share the knowledge you're learning, over time, you will find that you outgrow the conversations they're having and don't really love to participate in them. So bring them along; life is about impacting others and being a part of something greater than yourself. This will add gas to your tank and motivate you to keep moving the ball forward. When you see those you love win because you taught them something, there is no

> If you fail to share the knowledge you're learning, over time, you will find that you outgrow the conversations they're having and don't really love to participate in them.

greater reward. Share your growth by contributing financially to the charities you love or by helping someone you believe in get ahead in their business or investment goals.

Legacy is not just about the money.
It's also about the knowledge you leave behind.

"I had always encouraged my children and grandchildren to invest in real estate rather than rent. I donated the commission, and my children were responsible for the payments. Location was important, as was each child's lifestyle. My two youngest children preferred acreage and enjoyed keeping animals and gardens. My lawyer daughter's husband owned acreage, so I found homes in Phoenix for them. As I look back, I'm astounded by what we've done."

"Mike has had his duplex, a home in the country, a small ranchette rental, and a larger cattle ranch that he turned into a beautiful campground and event/retreat location for others to enjoy. Cheri has had her apartments and her lovely estate with an elegant historic home surrounded by a fruit orchard in Phoenix. Kerry has had multiple smaller ranches, one of which she sold part of for over $1 million as well as international getaways overlooking the beaches of Costa Rica. The grandkids were each given ten acres at the ranch when my husband, Jack, died. Logan and Jason sold part of theirs at once. Christin invested hers in a new house in Lake Havasu, which she sold for a profit, and she again invested in real estate. This has become a habit for her. Andrea bravely invested in a commercial property in Baltimore. It has appreciated. I gave the younger children, Andrea, Becky, Jack, Lauren, and Lillie, a 5 percent interest in my portion of our ranch. They have received $10,000 each and hopefully will get more."

"My investment criteria have always been location, price, terms, beauty, future appreciation, and water. My daughter Cheri and Larry's lovely house on two irrigated acres in Phoenix was priced at the height of their budget. However, the loan interest was much lower than comparable

property. It has been a fabulous home and appreciated from $500,000 to $1,300,000. Another property, a fixer-upper I found for Cheri and Larry, she was able to buy for $235,000. It sold for $1,600,000 after five years. It is a gorgeous antique house, and its location near Hance Park and museums helped considerably. Cheri put the house on the historical register, and I'm certain it will become a heritage home in downtown Phoenix."

"Often, we have had to solve problems that others avoid in order to acquire property. Kerry bought 160 acres (Soggy Bottom) at a very reasonable price and terms, but the railroad had closed the access under I40. She obtained permits over forest services and state land and has maintained that road for years. She did sell a portion of the property for over $1 million and will have at least that much value for the remainder."

—Grandma Clare

Financial freedom isn't just about your own comfort; it's also a path to transforming the lives of others. When you achieve this freedom, you hold the power to open doors of new opportunity, increased income, educational access, and free time so that others can experience personal growth and abundance as well. When they're free, they'll teach those around them to be free. The impact has a compound effect. This gift is your legacy, built on the blessings and support you've received.

Because others have lifted you, you have the responsibility to pay it forward and create a ripple effect of positive change for the people around you, just like those in the stories below have done.

> **Because others have lifted you, you have the responsibility to pay it forward and create a ripple effect of positive change for the people around you.**

Don & Carol:

At the beginning of the book, I shared a story about when my husband and I met Don and Carol. My husband was a contractor, and they came to us wanting to remodel their home. I'll never forget my husband telling me that Don was a perfectionist and that he didn't know how long he would be able to work for him—funny, coming from the mouth of a perfectionist. But they worked together and became each other's biggest fan.

One day, Don asked Mike about his goals and how business was going. Mike told him that we were working on our goal of building spec homes and funding the construction with hard money loans to the tune of 14 percent interest. Don cringed and told Mike he'd fund them for much less to help us out. You see, Don saw integrity and grit in a couple of kids trying to get ahead. We sat down for about fifteen minutes (the only time I ever met him in person), and he and his wife deposited $300,000 in our bank to move projects. I cried and remember wondering, "Who are these people who have done so well for themselves that they can deposit money like that into the account of a couple of kids they barely know?" They could never have imagined how that changed our lives forever. They literally changed the trajectory of future generations because they had the ability and the desire to bet on us financially. We paid it all back, of course, and have borrowed and paid it back over and over again for several years now.

About a year later, they needed a tax deduction and asked if they could help fund a college account for our kids. That moment changed me as a person. I realized that it was possible for me to build a life that could change generations just by loaning someone money to fund their ideas. I could empower people who never had the chance to bet on themselves to bet on their dreams. I knew that had to be my mission. Don has since passed, and we love his wife like family. We continue to check in and offer to help her in any way we can.

Your character will determine your opportunities.

"My first big sale came when I was giving my mother a bath. I postponed the client until the afternoon. He turned out to be a young man in his twenties who had visited some other realtors who didn't waste time on kids. He had three friends, all recent Annapolis graduates and naval officers, and they wanted to invest near Snowbowl. These young men bought 160 acres on the mountain and became friends and clients for several years. I took a 2 1/2 acre parcel of gorgeous mountain as part of my commission. Having a husband who supported the family

gave me the freedom to do that. I still own and treasure that land and the cabin we built there. Our family loves the cabin on the peaks. My son was married there fifty years ago, and I recently spent a few lovely and quiet weeks there, camping solo and still enjoying the beauty of nature at ninety-eight years of age."

—Grandma Clare

Life is all about relationships and impact. This is where happiness lives. It's a little like the story of Charles Dickens's character, Ebenezer Scrooge, in *A Christmas Carol*. He was a wealthy man with enough money to buy whatever he wanted, yet he was unhappy. When he discovered that giving and helping others brought him joy and changed their lives, happiness poured from him. He realized he mattered more than he knew and had the opportunity to make an impact that mattered on a big scale.

You can impact the world in so many ways! Often, it's those of us who have struggled who can best offer a hand up. Money is good for the good that it can do and is absolutely required if you want to bless many. Stop thinking money is the root of all evil and get excited about what it can do. The Bible says the *love* of money is the root of all evil; that's a different game (1 Timothy 6:10). Money is not evil; it only exposes character. If you are of good character, money will amplify and multiply your impact, character, and love for others. If you are of bad character, it will expose you. Focus on growing your wealth so that you can impact others. It's not about an obsession with money; it's about an obsession with freedom and impact!

> It's not about an obsession with money; it's about an obsession with freedom and impact!

Imagine something as simple as putting $5,000 in the S&P 500 right now for your 13-year-old child or grandchild, as I have done for my kids. It's as easy as using a free app like Robinhood and making transfers from your local bank. At an average 10 percent annual return over the last fifty years, if you simply auto-deposit $100 monthly, they will retire at sixty-five with more than $2.5 million. Using the "4 percent rule," if they withdrew it, that money would replace a $100,000 yearly salary for thirty years or $250,000 annually if they left it in and just lived off the growth. (The 4 percent rule of retirement states that you can spend 4 percent of your savings each year, and your retirement should last thirty years.)

You just planned their retirement! That's huge and simple! It's something anyone can do, yet almost no one does. If you were able to start with $15,000 and auto-deposit the same $100 per month, you would set them up with $160,000 per year or almost $4 million at retirement if they withdrew it. Instead of withdrawing it, however, a better plan would be to live off just the growth of that $4 million, which means they wouldn't use any of the original $4 million available at retirement. That would set them up with $400,000 per year and leave $4 million to pass on to their kids, their kids' kids, and on and on into the future while never taking a dollar from the actual $4 million. Even though the total amount invested was only $77,400, your children and grandchildren would live an abundant, six-figure lifestyle off the passive income generated from a single, simple decision you made on their behalf **(REFER TO THE INTEREST CALCULATOR RESOURCE AT THE END OF THIS CHAPTER)!** Building generational wealth is much less complicated than we think. It's a decision and a plan followed by simple, consistent action. That's it! Become a student of wealth, get the education, and take action. You owe it to those you love. Sharing knowledge changes lives!

Amanda:

I'll never forget mentoring my younger sister about investing. When she was just a kid, a great investment opportunity came up. I had found a home that was misclassified and priced much lower than it should have been. She had no credit and no money saved for a down payment, but I connected her to an expert who showed her how to build her credit in under six months. In the interim, we also found private financing until she could qualify for the mortgage. She took a chance and followed the plan when so many others had the opportunity but failed to execute.

She bought that house for just $60,000. After only five years, that home is worth almost $400,000! I didn't know it then, nor did she, but God knew she would spend time as a single mom, raising a beautiful boy and bringing in only one income. That tiny house payment amortized over thirty years was only a few hundred bucks a month, while rentals of the same size were three times that! I'm not sure she would have been able to do it alone. It would certainly have been much harder. She would need roommates or a second job, which would have stolen her time with her son.

She currently lives comfortably on her own and can choose to have a relationship because she wants one, not because she financially needs one. She will have her house paid for while she's still young and have the opportunity to leave a legacy for her son, pay for his college, or be available for him as he grows instead of working late hours. She currently has opportunities that would allow her to live in that house for free by boarding horses or having roommates. When I shared my knowledge, I had no idea it would change her life or future generations. What a blessing! She can now share the same knowledge with others. I could never have imagined the exponential impact of a single lesson.

Debbie:

My friend and broker was stuck in a busy career with high liability and much stress. She wanted the freedom to run her own business and travel but was under the thumb of an employer and not making enough money (or confident enough financially) to change that. One day, while looking for opportunities, I found a well-priced property that the seller would finance. After calling Deb, we ran through all the dos and don'ts and decided that if we could find a way to buy this home, it would bless her and give her son a place to live. She refinanced her home at a lower rate and pulled just enough for the down payment on this one. She secured a 4 percent rate with the seller over thirty years with no balloon payment and moved her son in as a tenant. She provided him with a safe, affordable place to live while gaining $700 per month cash flow and an appreciating asset. Once she realized how much fun that was, she had the courage to find a partner and do it again. Having the security of added monthly income, she has since started her own business with a flexible schedule and the ability to travel. She went from believing she would never be free from her job to building a life she loves in just a few short years. These are the things that make my heart happy!

Raelynn:

Raelynn's story is in her own words: "My introduction to real estate investing marked a significant shift in my mindset. Up until then, I viewed buying a home as just that—a home. The thought of purchasing a second, third, or even fourth property never crossed my mind. But when I started selling real estate and joined The Kingsbury Group, everything changed.

Christin is all about real estate investing. I remember one day at work when I was browsing the MLS for homes to invest in, and she asked sarcastically, 'Are you going to work or just look for investments to buy?'

I replied, 'Mmmm, look for investments.'

'Good,' she said. 'You'll make more money that way.'

I began by talking with a lender, and to my surprise, I got prequalified for a small amount because I was still nervous and wanted to borrow as little as possible. Eventually, I switched strategies, deciding to rent out my current home and buy a new one to live in. Personally, I think this is a great strategy. You can keep purchasing homes with minimal down payments while using the rental income to cover your mortgage and more.

Christin had a tremendous impact on my mindset, especially when it came to investments. I started reading books and talking to people about the best ways to approach this. I truly believe having the right mindset is crucial on this journey; it certainly was for me. I ended up buying a home in Prescott that needed some work but was priced well. My husband and I did all the renovations ourselves—it was mostly cosmetic—and we rented the house out for a great price. We sold our first home and used that money to save up and eventually buy another investment property in Tennessee, paying cash. By this point, we were earning enough profit to cover our household expenses.

At the beginning of 2023, I took a year-and-a-half break from selling real estate to stay home with my kids and focus on my family and church ministries. Without real estate, there's no way we would have been able to do this. The income from our properties provided the supplemental income needed to allow this change. Based on my experience, it amazes me that if money just sits there, it usually gets spent on random things, leaving nothing to show for it. But I was able to take advantage of the extra money I earned during my real estate years and put it into something lasting that contin-

> It amazes me that if money just sits there, it usually gets spent on random things, leaving nothing to show for it.

ues to benefit my family to this day."

Tracy:

Once again, with my eyes wide open, I was hunting for signs of distressed properties when I found a bank-owned property that needed a new owner. I brought it to the attention of my friend Tracy, who needed an affordable place to live. She picked it up with the help of her family.

This property provided her with a place to live and grew significantly in value over a few short years. She then turned it into a rental that produced a cash flow of almost $1,800 per month, providing their family with financial blessings and flexibility in their lives. Years later, they decided they no longer wanted to be landlords and sold that property, carrying the note. They continue to make awesome income by being the bank and earning interest on top of the payments and appreciation they have already earned.

Joel:

As I sit here today, I'm working with a young real estate agent I've mentored who has decided this industry isn't for him. He's tired of paying high rent and working like a dog all day at a restaurant to pay someone else's mortgage. With a bit of encouragement and relationships with the right people, he will buy his first house with almost nothing out of pocket, bring in a roommate to pay the mortgage and live for free. Not only is he living for free, but someone else is essentially buying the home for him.

It didn't require a bunch of money saved or a unique deal that couldn't be duplicated, just a relationship with someone who has gone before him, a real estate license that will give him a commission to use as a down payment, and a vision of where he wants to be. He will look back on this and see that this decision changed his entire life—a decision to build wealth for himself and his future rather than his landlord and theirs.

Kris & Bryce:

Nothing fills my cup more than helping young people build dreams! Kris and Bryce are both family and friends. Just five short years ago, I helped them buy a beautiful starter home within their budget and got them out of a rental where they were paying off someone else's mortgage.

With little money down and prior to kiddos, we made that dream a reality. It was not their dream home, but it was a beautiful home that they could comfortably afford, and it served them perfectly for five years. Most people buy what they dream of before they can afford it and are frustrated by the sacrifices it takes to keep it. These guys bought what they could afford and worked hard toward their dream home.

During those five years, babies were born, and memories were made. But just a month ago, they saw a gorgeous new home on the market in a beautiful, high-end neighborhood. It was what they had dreamed of, and it would be a blessing for their family, allowing their kids to ride bikes on quiet paved streets and attend better schools.

We made it happen by selling their first home, which provided the down payment for this new dream. Over $200,000 was earned in just five years by simply transitioning from renting to owning assets. That's more than many people make working forty hours a week over the course of a year, and it was nothing more than owning versus renting, coupled with the blessing of appreciation that real estate provides. I'm forever grateful for having the opportunity to help those I love build dreams and create wealth that impacts generations.

> That's more than many people make working forty hours a week over the course of a year, and it was nothing more than owning versus renting, coupled with the blessing of appreciation that real estate provides.

Josh & Kerri:

Just a few days ago, a young couple came to me because they had bought a house they really shouldn't have. It was beautiful but way over what they could comfortably afford. They had only owned it for a year, but it had created too much pressure on their marriage and finances. They felt pushed to work more and more, robbing them of family time and peace of mind. The good news was it had significantly appreciated in value, like real estate often does, growing by $300,000 in just over a year!

Selling it was going to cost them roughly $45,000 in capital gains taxes. Their plan was to sell and rent, which would cost them another $30,000 the following year in rent payments. Thinking on this, we discussed ways to defer the $45,000 and use the $30,000 to pay down their mortgage. This would also save them in tax write-offs and give them an appreciation of about $18,000.

A simple brainstorming session on how to stay in a home-ownership position, rather than becoming tenants, would bless them with over $93,000 in the first year alone. It would also keep them in an asset that appreciates and builds their net worth while costing no more than the rental they intended to move to. That's more than the average American family makes working forty hours a week for an entire year—but there was no work involved, just a decision to own versus rent!

People say knowledge is power, but how often do we walk blindly or emotionally uneducated and miss opportunities to change our future? We owe it to ourselves to study and have mentors in essential areas, such as our finances. We owe it to our kids to educate ourselves and change generations with that knowledge. This isn't something that only others know; this is something you need to know!

I could tell impact stories for days because they come up all the time and generally involve those I love most. My husband and I have had the opportunity to help many friends improve their financial positions. We have been blessed to teach them how to build passive income so that they can pursue what they truly love. They can now take the process and duplicate it again and again until their retirement plan and goals are funded.

People often tell me that they're not motivated by money. But I want you to remember that wealth provides freedom and flexibility to build a life on your terms. Money is just the tool used. You don't love

> **Wealth provides freedom and flexibility to build a life on your terms.**

the tool; you love what it can build that will bless others and move the mission forward. Financial freedom provides leverage and opportunity for others in your world. Leverage gives you back your time. So, if time and money equal *freedom*, then life on your terms requires an element of wealth, which will require you to be motivated by money to some extent. It's worth the time, the effort, and the sacrifice. Be proactive, not reactive. Take action now! Freedom and the ability to change lives and build generational wealth are the highest rewards for creating a life by design!

INTEREST CALCULATOR

You can use **FREE** tools to establish a forecast of your financial opportunities.

Initial Investment	$15,000
Annual Contribution	$0
Monthly Contribution	$100

Contribute at the ● beginning   end
of each compounding period

Rate of Return	10.00 %
Compound	annually
Investment length	52 years
Tax rate	0%
Inflation rate	3%

(sample)   CALCULATE

Possible *results!*

Ending balance	**$3,913,502.33**
Total principal	$77,400.00
Total contributions	$62,400.00
Total interest	**$3,836,102.33**
Interest of initial investment	$2,115,643.98
Interest of the contributions	$1,720,458.35
Buying power of the end balance after inflation adjustment	$841,453.09

What you Focus on *grows!*

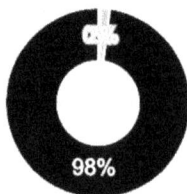

Initial investment
Contributions
Interest

98%

Chapter 21

START NOW

The best time to *start* was yesterday, but today will work just fine.

WHEN IT COMES DOWN TO THE DOING part, I find that most people will read and learn but get stuck when it comes to taking action. Generally, action is hindered by complexity or lack of time because we haven't prioritized it and cleared blocks on the calendar to focus on it. Let's break this down and make it so easy that you start now!

Ask yourself these questions:

- Now that I know what I know, what's stopping me?
- What do I need to start studying, and who can lead me?
- What can I simplify or get rid of to make time to prioritize my wealth journey?
- What options do I have that I haven't previously considered?
- What debts, payments, rates, and due dates do I currently have on my plate?
- What can I negotiate down?
- Can I combine high-rate debt into one bucket at a lower rate (without taking more money out)?
- Would that lower my payment so I could use the extra to pay down other debt or add to my emergency or investment buckets?
- What is most urgent? Why is it most urgent?
- Where could I focus energy that would increase income immediately?
- What things of value could I part with to raise capital for debt reduction and investment opportunities?

- What am I putting an emotional filter on that's clouding my vision and keeping me from making progress?
- What relationships or knowledge do I need to nurture and grow, or what relationships or knowledge am I missing completely?
- What's one thing that I can accomplish this week to make everything else on this journey easier or more fruitful?

Each week, ask yourself what's the *next best step*:

- Have a clear intention.
- Write down your daily goal.
- Time block it in your calendar.
- Always execute on the main priority.
- Measure, review, and adjust throughout the week if needed.
- Refuel physically and energetically and take breaks outside.
- Reward yourself.
- Make a promise and follow through.

> **My greatest wish is that you take this information, believe in yourself, find the environment and people you need around you, and literally change your life!**

As you turn the final page, know that my greatest wish is that you take this information, believe in yourself, find the environment and people you need around you, and literally change your life! In life, there are people who learn and others who take what they learn, put it into action, and come out completely changed. You have the ability; you have the information. Make the commitment to change your world and, in turn, change the worlds of those around you **(REFER TO THE STAY MOTIVATED RESOURCE AT THE END OF THIS CHAPTER).** Your journey doesn't end here; this is only the beginning. The strategies and steps you have learned are your foundation, but the true power lies in your next move. Imagine the opportunities you will unlock, the legacy you will build, and the freedom you will achieve. I can't wait to hear the stories and see the lives you impact because you decided to be different.

Stay Motivated

You have heard the saying "Your willpower is not on will call." Feelings will come and go, so we can't depend on feelings to get us to our goal. We must be intentional about creating a motivating environment and self.

SET CLEAR GOALS

Set Clear Goals: Define specific, achievable goals that excite you. Having a clear target gives you something to work toward and helps you stay motivated.

BREAK THINGS INTO SMALL BITES

Break Tasks into Smaller Steps: Divide your goals into smaller, manageable tasks. Completing these smaller steps can provide a sense of accomplishment and keep you motivated as you progress.

REMEMBER WHY

Find Your "Why": Understand why your goals matter to you. Identify the personal or emotional reasons behind your objectives; this deeper connection can boost motivation.

INTENTIONALLY INSPIRE YOURSELF

Stay Inspired: Surround yourself with inspiration. Whether it's reading success stories, watching motivational videos, or being around supportive people, constant inspiration can keep your motivation levels high.

GIVE YOURSELF A TREAT

Reward Yourself: Celebrate your achievements, even the small ones. Rewards can reinforce positive behavior and make the journey toward your goals more enjoyable. Remember that motivation can ebb and flow, so it's essential to continually revisit and adjust these strategies as needed.

AFTERWORD

CHRISTIN IS WISE BEYOND HER YEARS BECAUSE she seeks advice (Grandma Clare) and takes action. Taking action has placed her financially far beyond most her age. My relationship with Christin has allowed me to witness her personal sacrifices in serving others while demonstrating what it is to be a servant leader.

My personal focus is on leadership, specifically Leading a Life Well Lived. The essence of each person's life is captured in five interconnected areas: Spiritual, Personal, Family, Financial, and Community. In this book, Chistin has ventured into each one of these areas, teaching the correct way of thinking, planning, and acting to experience a Life Well Lived.

I believe that each one of us is perfectly positioned to receive what we are currently receiving in life based on how we think, the environment we create or allow around us, and the people we spend time with. When we change how we think, we change what we choose to do, and we change what we get. Thinking is a spiritual transaction. Thoughts cannot be seen or touched, but they are real. In this book, Christin has told us how she thinks and what she does to achieve what she has.

Many just make plans for themselves and maybe for their immediate family. Leading a life well lived requires clarity on your values, your rules for living, and your vision for what abundance in each area of life looks like. Christin's acronym for financial freedom, F+A+M+I+L+Y (Chapter 15), is wisdom. You know it. You felt it when you were reading, but don't just read it; study it and then implement it into your life. When you think about what she shared (the family bank concept), it is clear that she is still at it, adding value not just to her current but to her future family members as well.

Christin has shared a productive way of thinking. When you change how you think, you'll change what you do. The tools she has provided will help you do the right things. When you commit to doing those things you will change the outcomes in your life well lived.

Thank you, Christin, for blessing others.

Steve Chader
Author of *HOLD*, Musician, Investor, Teacher

INDEX

ABOUT THE AUTHOR

Christin Kingsbury is a God-loving mother of two littles, a wife, the CEO of a small million-dollar real estate team, and a founding partner of PLACE, a partnership of top agents across the country.

She is the owner of several real estate-related businesses and investment properties. She has built and acquired complementary businesses that create multiple streams of income from a single transaction. These range from brokerages and title companies to a mobile home park and short and long-term rentals, most of which were secured using relationships and creative financing with little to no money out of pocket. Over the years, she has built and held multifamily properties, flipped single-family homes, developed land, and built spec homes. Currently, she is building out a destination campground and retreat center.

She is passionate about the security and opportunity that passive income brings to families during times like these. She wants families to live life on their terms, filled with adventure and amazing experiences rather than being bound by the traditional finance world. She has coauthored a best seller on integrating faith, family, and passive income, built a multi-million-dollar net worth, carries zero consumer debt, and holds only assets that pay for themselves, all generating income that is twice the cost of owning them.

She teaches others how to get out of debt, create multiple streams of income, and use their abundance to bless others. Her goal is to empower believers to use their talents to lift up others by teaching them to self-fund their missions.

She believes that educating people to make new choices around money can break old poverty mindsets and build generational wealth. Her companies work daily to fund financial and business education for at-risk kids and break generational curses of financial scarcity that challenge and destroy marriages and the family unit.

Book worksheets

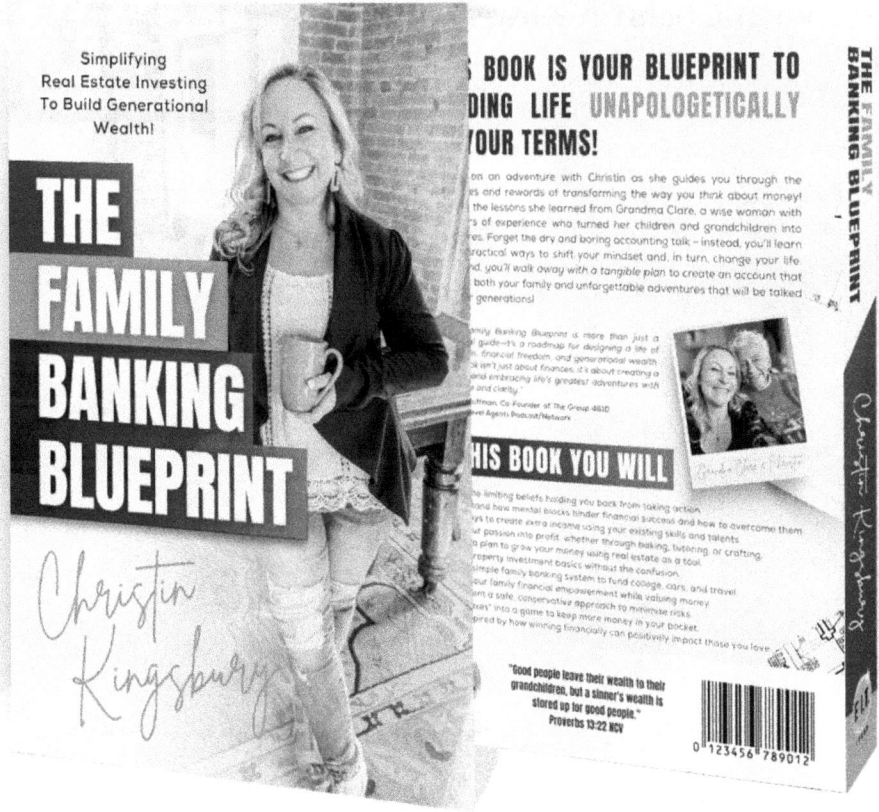

SCAN HERE

Simplifying Real Estate Investing To Build Generational Wealth!

THE FAMILY BANKING BLUEPRINT

Christin Kingsbury

S BOOK IS YOUR BLUEPRINT TO
DING LIFE UNAPOLOGETICALLY
OUR TERMS!

on an adventure with Christin as she guides you through the
es and rewards of transforming the way you think about money!
the lessons she learned from Grandma Clare, a wise woman with
s of experience who turned her children and grandchildren into
es. Forget the dry and boring accounting talk – instead, you'll learn
actical ways to shift your mindset and, in turn, change your life.
d, you'll walk away with a tangible plan to create an account that
both your family and unforgettable adventures that will be talked
generations!

mily Banking Blueprint is more than just a
guide—it's a roadmap for designing a life of
n, financial freedom, and generational wealth
k isn't just about finances; it's about creating a
and embracing life's greatest adventures with
e and clarity."

ffman, Co-Founder of The Group 4610
vel Agents Podcast/Network

HIS BOOK YOU WILL

he limiting beliefs holding you back from taking action
and how mental blocks hinder financial success and how to overcome them
ys to create extra income using your existing skills and talents
ur passion into profit, whether through baking, tutoring, or crafting
a plan to grow your money using real estate as a tool
roperty investment basics without the confusion
our family banking empowerment while valuing money
g banking system to fund college, cars, and travel
ant a safe, conservative approach to minimize risks
xes" into a game to keep more money in your pocket
pired by how winning financially can positively impact those you love

"Good people leave their wealth to their
grandchildren, but a sinner's wealth is
stored up for good people."
Proverbs 13:22 NCV

0 123456 789012

Scan to access all the worksheets from inside
this book that Christin has created for you!

Connect with Christin

Friend + Follow + Connect
with Christin Kingsbury

SCAN HERE

Let's get you
INVESTING

SCAN HERE

It's never too late or too early to start!
Let's get you investing!

Freebie!

FREE
Wealth
Series
Text
"Assets"
to
59559

Freedom number
CALCULATOR

SCAN HERE

Scan to learn your "real" needs for retirement with access to the freedom number calculator!

Join our next Wealth Building Mastermind Adventure Retreat!
Text "**RETREAT**" to **59559**

WEALTH BUILDING
adventure retreat!

Ready to ditch the grind and refresh the excitement and possibility of your future? Join us on an epic adventure retreat—where profitable business owners like you break free from the exhausting hustle, unlock money-multiplying habits, and forge game-changing connections! Step out of your comfort zone, design your abundance blueprint, and team up with like-minded trailblazers who'll keep you on track. Surrounded by God's jaw-dropping creation, you'll reset, recharge, and dive into business-boosting education and creative masterminding. **Say YES to freedom, fresh opportunities, and relationships that open doors!**

Guest Speaker

SCAN HERE

Scan to invite Christin to guest speak on your podcast, zoom, or at your next event!

F. I.T.

PRESS

Your story doesn't just matter for you, it matters to move others!

1 CHRONICLES 16:24 (NLT)
Publish His glorious deeds among the nations.
Tell everyone about the amazing things he does.

A Christian Publishing House dedicated to turning messages into movements. On mission to mobilize the critical voices for such a time as this. Specializing in co-hort compilations, to make way for writers to collaborate with other prolific members of the Body of Christ. Our works open conversations around mental, physical, relational, financial and spiritual health and wholeness journeys, often directly associated to our rooted identity and purpose driven life.

Learn More & Don't Wait to Get Published!

www.ingramcontent.com/pod-product-compliance
Lightning Source LLC
Chambersburg PA
CBHW071416210326
41597CB00020B/3529